Basic Knowledge
Higher English

John O'Neill

ROBERT GIBSON · PUBLISHER

17 FITZROY PLACE GLASGOW G3 7SF

INTRODUCTION

The Examination Board is currently engaged in reviewing the whole nature of the Higher English examination, and is seeking the views of the English teaching profession and other interested parties before deciding what form any new examination should take. This is a process which will take some years, and in the meantime some 35 000 candidates each year must prepare themselves for the examination as it exists at present. Such people will hardly need to be reminded of the importance of this examination. The 'Highers' are the recognised final school qualification in Scotland, used as the basis of selection for all forms of higher education and most professional careers. Of all the subjects examined, English attracts by far the largest number of candidates, and it can truthfully be said that without a pass in this subject entry to many very worthwhile careers is totally barred. This probably accounts for the enormous increase in the number of candidates in recent years, and particularly in the number of adult as distinct from school candidates.

When this book originally appeared in 1973, it drew all of its illustrative examples from the examinations set in 1970 and 1971. Since these papers are no longer readily available, it has been revised in such a way as to draw its examples chiefly from 1978 and 1979, with only a few references to slightly earlier papers. At the same time attention has been paid to various slight changes which have occurred over the years in the format of the papers and the style of questioning.

The book is addressed directly to the student himself, but it is hoped that many teachers will also find in it much that will be useful in preparing their candidates. Although based exclusively on the S.C.E. syllabus and examination, it could also prove useful to students of English at any other level, since it deals with most aspects of English as a subject of school study.

J.O'N.
August, 1980

CONTENTS

The Basic Approach

Composition

Interpretation and Language

Literature

Some Reminders

Appendix

THE BASIC APPROACH

The Importance of Higher English

Probably no reader of this book will require to be told how important is the S.C.E. examination in Higher English. In Scotland, the S.C.E. examinations are the standard means of entry to universities and other forms of higher education, and they are also used extensively as a means of selection for many worthwhile careers. English is a particularly important subject, since most authorities stipulate English as one of the passes which are required for a successful application. The number of candidates in Higher English is itself an indication of its importance – currently about 35 000. Of these, about 5 000 are candidates from Further Education Colleges or candidates who have entered privately. This latter figure represents an enormous number of people who, having left school without this qualification, have come to realise what they have missed and are now working hard to gain a second chance in life.

It is perhaps not so widely realised, however, that in many cases merely to pass in Higher English is not enough. There are three grades of pass – A(70%), B(60%), and C(50%). Entrance requirements for courses at universities and other institutions are very complex, but generally they demand a certain number of passes at A or B grades, and English is one of the subjects frequently stipulated. It follows, therefore, that for all but the most gifted candidates a great deal of effort is required to ensure that the result achieved is the best possible. The chapters which follow will, it is hoped, be of some help to all readers.

The Examination Syllabus

Each year, in its publication "Conditions and Arrangements" the Examination Board includes for each subject the syllabus under which the examination will be held. The syllabus may vary on minor matters

9

from time to time, but no major alterations are made without several years' notice.

The English examination consists of three papers, to be taken by all candidates.

Paper I – Composition – 1 hour 40 minutes – 50 marks.
Paper II – Interpretation and Language – 1 hour 30 minutes – 50 marks.
Paper III – Literature – 1 hour 50 minutes – 60 marks.

Paper I consists of two questions both of which must be answered. In Question A *(normally either 30 or 35 marks)*, candidates are asked to choose one from a number of themes and write a substantial composition on it. Several different modes of writing are offered: narrative, descriptive, reflective essay; discussion, diary, debate, speech, article, letter, etc. Candidates are expected to write in a style which is appropriate to the mode they have chosen. In Question B *(usually 15 or 20 marks)* there is no choice. A body of information is supplied, and candidates are expected to evaluate the comparative importance of the different items of information, and to compose an answer in continuous formal prose using those parts of the given material which they consider relevant and adopting a tone appropriate to the instructions and to the nature of the material.

Paper II also consists of two compulsory questions. Question A *(approximately 40 marks)* tests the candidates' understanding of a piece of prose of moderate difficulty. Various possible areas of questioning may be involved: the meaning of words, phrases and sentences: the inter-relation of ideas; summarising; appropriateness of language; grammatical structure and usage; the conventions of written English. Not all of these areas of competence will necessarily be tested every year. Question B *(approximately 10 marks)* tests awareness of the features of different varieties of English, and candidates are expected to observe the ways in which a difference of purpose in the use of language leads to differences in typography, vocabulary, structure, grammatical form, etc.

Paper III consists of four sections – Drama, Prose, Poetry and Practical Criticism. Candidates are required to answer three questions, each chosen from a different section of the paper. Each question carries 20 marks. In Sections 1, 2 and 3, candidates are required to select texts appropriate to the question asked, to show some detailed knowledge of the texts chosen, to organise that knowledge in the form of description or argument, and to communicate in an appropriate style their own impressions of the texts chosen. Section 4 (Practical Criticism) is normally based on a poem. Questions are set on this text designed to test understanding of the meaning, appreciation of the manner in which it is written, and the candidates' ability to express their own responses to the text.

Later chapters will consider each of the three papers in turn, and will try to show exactly what is implied by the different parts of this syllabus.

Use of Past Papers

The best way to realise what the syllabus means in terms of the examination itself is, of course, to inspect the papers which have actually been set. Single copies of these papers can be bought, but much more useful is the book of past papers published by Gibson. No better practice material exists, and these papers will be referred to throughout this book.

The Nature of the Subject

English as a subject for study and examination is different from most other subjects. It is a subject in which the student has to acquire not knowledge so much as skill – a practical subject, to be compared with Art and Music rather than with Chemistry and Geography. A great deal of knowledge is required, of course, but it is not a body of factual knowledge to be memorised as part of a course of study; rather it is an awareness of the conventions of language which has been assimilated in the course of a lifetime. There are many lists of facts which *could* be memorised – definitions of figures of speech, rules of spelling with exceptions to the rules, different uses of the comma, prefixes and suffixes with their derivation and meaning, and many more. But it is not knowledge of these facts on which you will be examined; it is the ability to make use of the knowledge in your writing, and to recognise in your reading the ways in which others have used their knowledge.

The development of the necessary skill in reading and writing is a slow process, and not one which can readily be accelerated in a "crammers" course. It is a development which began for all of us in infancy and which continues throughout our lives. No student of English starts off without knowledge. Most of the knowledge required is there already, waiting to be brought to the surface. What can be done in a book such as this is perhaps to fill a few gaps in the existing knowledge, but chiefly to offer help in using to the best advantage the knowledge that is already there.

The most important thing to realise about English is that it is the language as it really exists, in all its varieties. The notion of "good" English which must be learned and "bad" English which must be unlearned must be discarded. English is "good" if it is appropriate to the user and the situation, "bad" if it is inappropriate. The language of the child in the playground, the teenager in the disco, the fan on the terracing,

11

the housewife in the laundrette is "good" if it is understood and accepted in its situation, but would not necessarily be "good" if used by the minister from the pulpit, or the teacher in front of a class, or the lawyer in a letter to client, or the scientist in his description of an experiment. Every situation has its own appropriate language, and English is only "bad" English when it is used inappropriately. What the English student must do is try to observe the different varieties of English in use, and choose at all times the language best suited to the situation. At all times – and not just when he claims to be studying English – he must listen and read with awareness of the differences he observes, and speak and write with consciousness of the choices he makes and the reasons for his choices.

In the field of literature, too, there has been a change of attitude over recent years. No longer should the English student believe that there is a body of great works which must be known and revered regardless of the enjoyment or otherwise they may offer. Such great works do of course exist, but the Higher English examination is not concerned solely with such books. It is concerned with the genuineness with which the candidate responds to what he has read, the degree of understanding he reveals, and the skill with which he can express this. The better the book, the more opportunity it will provide for deep and sensitive response on the part of the student, but there is no book that every student should feel an obligation to enjoy. The candidate who has never managed to understand any work of great depth but who says genuinely what his reading has meant to him will fare much better than one who prepares in advance a set of opinions which he does not sincerely hold but which he thinks will satisfy the examiner. Thus there are no "good" books and "bad" books in absolute terms. A "good" book is one which the student can understand and which gives him some degree of pleasure and enlightenment; a "bad" book is one which he fails to understand and which leaves him entirely unaffected.

The Student's Attitude

In the light of what has been said, it is obviously impossible to offer a cut-and-dried course in English which will guarantee examination success. What, then, is the best way for the student to proceed?

Quite simply, he must expose himself as much as possible to English in use. He must read all he can – and not just "Literature". Magazines and newspapers, both serious and trivial, letters, notices, advertisements, application forms are just as much part of English as plays, novels and poems, and all should be read critically. He must write too – and not just formal essays. He should, of course, practise his essay-writing, but he should also write about the books he reads, he should perhaps keep a diary, he should try his hand at composing poetry, he should write letters, he should write simply for pleasure. All of this writing should be subjected to close examination, with a view to observing how appropriate it is, how clear, how well it fulfils its purpose. Intelligent listening and talking are also part of the English training, since these activities can reveal some fundamental differences between the spoken and written forms of the language. In short, the best way to learn English is to use it.

This is the best way to become proficient in the use of English, but there remains the question of passing the examination. For this it will not be enough merely to cultivate the good habits which have been described. The candidate who is proficient at English will possibly pass even without specific training in examination technique, but he may not achieve the grade of pass which he is capable of achieving. In order to do as well as possible it is necessary to become thoroughly aware of what is being tested and of some of the pitfalls which lie in wait.

For this purpose, later chapters will deal with the different aspects of the paper, explaining what is expected of the candidate and suggesting programmes of work. All three parts of the English paper – Composition, Interpretation and Language, and Literature – are part of the one subject. There are no barriers between them. When we read, we are learning to write; when we write an essay, we are developing our ability to interpret other people's writing. It is convenient for the purposes of this book to treat the different aspects of the examination separately, but this is purely a matter of convenience. The basic method of preparation is the same for all parts – listen and talk, read and write.

What is offered here is not a systematic course, to be studied progressively from cover to cover. Such a course is, as already explained, not feasible. The different sections are offered separately, but should be studied concurrently. The amount of time and concentration spent on any one section will depend on the needs of the student and judgement of the teacher.

As has already been explained, there is no body of knowledge which must be systematically learned. Nevertheless, if we are to observe English profitably and, as a result of our observation, to use it effectively, we must have at least some understanding of the nature of the language, and some terminology with which to discuss it. In the rest of this chapter, some attempt will be made to provide this. It will not be a set of rules of good English, merely a brief and necessarily incomplete description of the language as it is used. Ideally it should be read through quickly and then referred to from time to time as the need arises. If no such need arises, then this section can be largely ignored. The information it contains is not to be regarded as an essential ingredient of a Higher English course; it is merely a reference section.

An Introduction to Grammar

For centuries school pupils being taught English were trained in a traditional set of grammatical rules which were considered essential to the learning of good English. There was a very narrow idea as to what constituted good English, and every departure from this idea was considered to be a positive error. Some time ago, however, several research findings revealed that there is virtually no carry-over from the learning of grammatical rules into the student's own speech and writing. Indeed, to spend much time on such rules has been shown to be a possible barrier to the production of effective English. As a result, a reaction set in, and for some years virtually no grammar was taught at all. Nowadays the truth is seen by most to lie between these two extremes. There has been a realisation that the old rules of prescription ("You must do this") and proscription ("You must not do that") should be replaced simply by description of what actually happens when language is used.

The need for description rather than prescription or proscription is most clearly seen when we become aware of the enormous variety of English that can be found. Traditional grammar holds good only for one tiny sector of English, the formal literary style. But even this needs qualification. Literary English changes considerably from age to age, and even in one period many reputable authors, who should be our best exponents of the language, depart frequently and deliberately from what is considered the norm. The newspapers, which are the chief model of written English for the majority of people, depart radically from the norm, and even among newspapers, there are many variations in usage. Spoken English has different conventions from any form of written English. British English is very different (not merely in pronunciation but in vocabulary and grammar) from American, West Indian and Australian English, for example; indeed British English is only a tiny fragment of the whole language as it is used by native speakers of English throughout the world, and there is no reason to suppose that it is in any way superior to the English which is the native language of many other countries. Even British English varies from region to region, from person to person, and from situation to situation. It is obviously absurd to imagine that there is one brand of the language which can be said without qualification to be correct.

14

Before we can talk about English at all, however, we must have some agreed conventions on which to base our discussion. For that reason only – and not for its own sake – the following description of English is offered. It is by no means complete and detailed. It is merely a much simplified explanation of one acceptable way of looking at English. It is not the only way, perhaps not even the best way, but it is reasonably simple and reasonably accurate. The terminology may be strange to many, and it may conflict in places with other better-known terminologies, but since in this field there is no universal agreement it may prove acceptable for the present purpose. This whole field is very specialised, and for some time to come it must remain the concern of departments of linguistics in the universities. In the meantime, however, the layman and the schools need something to be going on with, and perhaps this will serve for the present.

Four Basic Concepts of Grammar

There are four basic concepts of grammar – Unit, Structure, Class and System.

Unit: There are five units of grammar, named here in descending order of rank:

> Sentence
> Clause
> Group
> Word
> Morpheme

Each of these units, except the lowest, can be defined in terms of the unit below. Thus the Sentence consists of Clauses, the Clause of Groups, the Group of Words and the Word of Morphemes. Consider, for example, the following:

> When I talked to him on the phone, he told me that the latest consignment would arrive in the evening.

This is a sentence. It is made up of three clauses:

> When I talked to him on the phone
> he told me
> that the latest consignment would arrive in the evening.

Within each clause there is a series of groups:

> on the phone
> the latest consignment
> in the evening.

Note however, that some groups – 'he', for example – can consist of single words. Each group, therefore, is made up of one or more words. The morpheme is the lowest unit. Some words are themselves morphemes, since they cannot be further subdivided, but others consist of more than one grammatical unit. 'Talked', for example, has two morphemes, 'talk' and '-ed'.

Special note should be made of the so-called 'phrasal verbs'. Here what appears to be a group of words is really the expression of a single notion, and the expression should be regarded as a word, not a group. Examples are common in everyday speech – to check up on, to put up with, to ask for, etc.

Notice also that a single expression may operate simultaneously at several different ranks. For example:

> Are you coming out? – No.

'No' is a sentence, a clause, a group, a word and a morpheme all at once.

> Where were you last night? – In the house.

'In the house' is a sentence, a clause and a group all at once.

Structure: Each unit except the smallest, the morpheme, has a structure which can be described in terms of the unit below it. Thus sentence structure can be described in terms of its component clauses and their relationship with each other, as in the process known as general analysis (Clause, Kind, Relation). Word structure can be described in terms of morphemes, as in the example 'talked' already mentioned, which consists of the lexical (or meaningful) item 'talk' plus the grammatical item '-ed', which is the verbal ending in the past tense. Clause structure and group structure are more complex and must be treated more fully.

The four elements of clause structure are S, P, C, A (Subject, Predicator, Complement, Adjunct). These four elements are best defined by example:

S	P	C	A
The grocer	/ packed	/ the goods	/ in a large box.
He	/ will send	/ them	/ this afternoon.
I	/ shall check	/ everything	/ very carefully.

Note that the element C includes both the Direct Object and Indirect Object of traditional grammar:

S	P	C	C	A
He	/ will send	/ me	/ the bill	/ later.

SPCA is the normal word order in English, though it can be altered for various reasons. For example, special emphasis can be achieved by placing an item out of its expected place:

C	S	P
This	/ I	/ know

Several adjuncts may be present in one clause, and for purposes of balance they may be placed in different positions:

A	S	P	C	A
Next week	/ I	/ shall send	/ another order	/ to the grocer.

Sometimes it is not possible to say whether an item is S or C. In such cases it is called Z:

S	P	Z	P	C
I	/ saw	/ him	/ crossing	/ the road

'Him' is C of 'saw' and S of 'crossing', therefore it is labelled Z.

Normally the places SPCA in the clause are filled by groups (or words which are themselves groups). In some cases, however, one of these places is filled by a clause operating at the rank of group. When this occurs we may call it a rank-shifted clause.

S	P	C
That he should run away	/ is	/ incredible.

There are different types of group structure, depending on the function of the group. Thus the adverbial group operating at A may consist of the preposition followed by the object it governs – 'in a large box', 'to the grocer', for example. Verbal groups may be defined in terms of auxiliary verb and root verb – 'may go', 'have been thinking', etc. The group whose structure most requires examination is the nominal group – the item S, C, or that part of the adverbial group at A which follows the preposition. The main word of the nominal group, the word which fulfils the naming function, is the headword (h). Any item which precedes it is the modifier (m), and any item which follows it is the qualifier (q). Thus the structure of the nominal group can be described as:

     (m) h (q)

For example:

h		
He		
m	h	
The old	/ man	
m	h	q
The old	/ man	/ with the stick

The modifier may consist of several parts, and when this happens they occur in a fixed order, though they are all simply labelled as adjectives in some grammars. These adjectives can be broken into four different types: articles, or determiners (d); numbers, or ordinals (o); descriptive adjectives, or epithets (e); and noun-adjectives (n). For example:

d	o	e	n	h
The	/ three	/ new	/ glass	/ jars.

This order – d, o, e, n – is almost invariably maintained in the modifier of a nominal group. If there are several epithets they are normally separated by commas:

     The three new, fragile, green glass jars.

A heavy use of modifiers and qualifiers is often a feature of advertising language and of newspaper headlines, especially the use of the noun-adjective:

     £10m Border Development Plan Setback
     Every packet carries a Government Health Warning.
     Top quality value-for-money bargain offers!

Class: Units of language can be put into classes in many different ways. For example, the unit "word" can be classified according to the Parts of Speech – noun, pronoun, verb, adjective, adverb, conjunction, preposition, interjection. Groups can be classified according to type – nominal group operating at S or C, verbal group operating at P, adverbial group operating at A. Clauses can be classified as independent or dependent, and dependent clauses can be further classified according to their function in the sentence. Consider the following example:

S	P	C	A
I	/ shall make	/ a cup of tea	/ when you come home.

This is a sentence which consists of two clauses:

> I shall make a cup of tea
> when you come home

The first clause is independent; the second is dependent on the first. Within the whole sentence the second clause operates as an adjunct. It can therefore be classified as a dependent adverbial clause.

Sentences can be classified according to mood, of which there are three. The affirmative mood expresses a statement:

> He will come back

The interrogative mood expresses a question:

> Will he come back?

The imperative mood expresses a command:

> Come back.

There is also a fourth mood, the subjunctive, but this is found only in a few survivals of this archaic form:

> If only he were here.

These are the most important classifications of the various units. Certain sub-classifications can also be made. Adverbs and adverbial groups can be sub-classified as adverbs of time, place, manner etc. Nouns can be described as abstract or concrete; common or proper; collective; masculine, feminine or neuter. These sub-classifications are of little or no grammatical value. The distinction between common and proper noun, e.g., is important only in that the proper noun begins with a capital letter and the common noun with a small letter. The only significant point about the collective noun is that it is normally thought of as being a singular item rather than plural, so that we say that a flock of sheep *is* grazing rather than *are* grazing. On the other hand, many collective nouns are often thought of as being plural:

> The committee have made their decision.
> The BBC are showing a series of repeats this summer.

At one time such uses would have been thought of as being in error, but now they are regarded as being simply a fact of language, neither right nor wrong. The other distinctions – abstract or concrete; masculine, feminine or neuter – are simply matters of meaning, not of grammar.

System: The term 'system' is given to any form of grammatical choice made from a limited number of possibilities. Thus we have, for example, positive as opposed to negative, singular as opposed to plural. In using a noun, we choose between singular and plural according to a system. If the noun we are using is 'boy' but we require the plural form, we achieve this by adding the morpheme '-s' to the singular form. We do not find, however, "The boys is playing in the street." The item S, 'the boys', is in the plural and so the verb will also appear in its plural form, 'are playing'.

Another system is that of tense in the verb. We choose to say either 'is playing' or 'was playing' according to the sense which we wish to convey. Some languages (French, for example) have a very complex system of tenses in which the form of the verb varies in many different ways. In English, however, there are basically only two tenses, the present and the past. When we want to use what in other languages may be described as, say, the future, the pluperfect, the future perfect, or the imperfect tenses, we simply use a combination which consists of the present or past tense of the verbs 'to be', 'to have', or certain auxiliary verbs together with either the infinitive, the present participle, or the past participle of the root verb.

For Example:

I walk	Present tense
I walked	Past tense
I shall walk	Present tense 'shall' + Infinitive
I had walked	Past tense 'had' + Past participle
I shall have been walking	Present tense 'shall' + Present tense 'have' + Past participle 'been' + Present participle 'walking'.

Yet another system of English is the system of case. In some languages, again, the case system is very complex. In Latin, for example, there are six different cases of the noun, depending on the function of the noun in the sentence, and the noun ending is altered in order to fit the case chosen, and also to fit the number, since there is a separate set of case endings for the plural. The user of Latin, therefore, has to determine which case is appropriate to the situation and choose the correct form from quite a long list of possibilities. In English, however, the case system applies in a very limited way. In the noun, the only case variation is that between the nominative and possessive cases (boy/boy's; boys/boys'). In the pronoun there is one important case distinction. The nominative case of the personal pronoun is 'I', 'he', 'she', 'we', 'you', 'they'. When the personal pronoun is used other than as the subject of a verb, a different case form is used, called variously objective or accusative case:

Nominative		Accusative
I	saw	him
He	saw	me
We	saw	her
They	saw	us
You	saw	them

The pronoun 'who' also shares this case system:

Who told you so?
By *whom* were you told?

The system of gender is another which is quite complex in some languages but very simple in English. In the noun the system of gender does not exist at all. We do not alter the noun ending in order to make a distinction between masculine and feminine, nor do we have to make the endings of other words such as adjectives agree with the gender of the noun concerned. The only gender system we have is in the personal pronoun, where we choose 'he', 'she' or 'it' in order to suit the noun to which the pronoun refers.

In the verb there is the system of 'person' – first person, the person speaking; second person, the person spoken to; and third person, the person or thing spoken about. In most verbs, the only distinction is in the third person in the singular form. Thus, I talk, you talk, we talk, they talk – but he *talks*. In the same way, I think but he *thinks*. In the verb 'to be' the system of choice is slightly wider: we are, you are, they are – but I *am* and he *is*. In all verbs there is also an archaic form of the second person singular which still appears in certain situations – thou art, thou hast, thou gavest, etc.

One other system may be mentioned, that of the comparison of adjectives. Here there are three degrees of comparison – positive, comparative and superlative:

| old | older | oldest |
| young | younger | youngest |

Many of these, of course, are formed in ways other than by the addition of an ending. One such example is:

| good | better | best |

By using the four basic concepts of grammar – Unit, Structure, Class, System – it is possible to describe whatever occurs in any piece of English.

Under each heading we can list some of the things which might be said. Consider, for example, the following:

> My youngest son is going to sea as soon as he leaves school.

Unit: This is a sentence.

It contains two clauses — My youngest son is going to sea as soon as he leaves school.

The clauses consist of groups — My youngest son
is going
to sea
as soon as
he
leaves
school.

The whole item consists of words.
Some of the words contain two morphemes — young-est
go-ing
leave-s

Structure:

The whole sentence has the pattern SPAA

S   P   A   A
My youngest son / is going / to sea / as soon as he leaves school.

The sentence consists of two clauses, the second dependent on the first and operating at A in the sentence.

The second clause consists of a subordinator or binder 'as soon as' followed by SPC.

'My youngest son' is a nominal group operating at S.

It consists of a modifier, 'My youngest', and a headword, 'son'. The modifier consists of determiner, 'My', and epithet, 'youngest'. 'Youngest' consists of two morphemes, 'young' and '-est'.

'to sea' is an adverbial group operating at A.

'school' is a word in the clause 'as soon as he leaves school' operating at C in that clause.

Class:

'son', 'sea' and 'school' are nouns.
'is going' and 'leaves' are verbs.
'he' is a pronoun replacing 'My youngest son'.

'youngest' is an adjective.
'as soon as he leaves school' is a dependent adverbial clause of time.
The sentence is in the affirmative mood.

System:
'is going' is positive.
'son' and 'he' are singular.
The verbs 'is going' and 'leaves' are also singular agreeing with their subjects.
'is going' and 'leaves' are in the present tense.
'is going' consists of the present tense 'is' plus the present participle 'going'.
'he' is in the nominative case.
'he' is masculine gender.
'leaves' is in the third person, agreeing with 'he'.
'youngest' is the superlative form of young'.
Two particular items may be isolated for a full description:

youngest: This item consists of two morphemes.
It is a word.
It forms part of a nominal group operating at S.
It functions within the group as an epithet in the modifier of the headword.
It is an adjective.
It is a superlative adjective.

school: This item is a morpheme.
It is also a word.
It is also a group.
It is a nominal group.
It consists of a headword only.
It operates at C in its clause.
It is part of a clause which operates at A in the sentence.
It is a noun.
It is singular.

The sentence which has been used here as an example is, of course, relatively uncomplicated, but the method of description can be applied to any case. It would not be wise at this stage, however, to discuss some of the complexities which may arise. To do so would probably only cause confusion. Such complexities as may occur in the Higher English papers will be dealt with later in the appropriate places.

The Concept of Register

Something has already been said about the many different varieties of English which can be found. It is now time to say a little more about this. First of all, there is a convenient term which may be used as a short-cut when we discuss this subject – the term 'register'. This is the name we give to any variety of English which can be recognised as having its own distinguishing characteristics. Those characteristics are themselves sometimes described as the 'markers' of a particular register.

There are some obvious examples of this. We can readily observe the fact that in most scientific writing there is a much more frequent use of the passive voice of the verb than occurs in most other forms of English:

> Water was heated to boiling point.
> It was observed that . . .

In other registers we would find

> I heated the water . . .
> I observed . . .

The use of the passive voice, then, could be said to be one of the markers of the scientific register. It is not the only marker of that register of course. It would also be true to say that the scientific register is invariably formal and impersonal and contains a high proportion of technical language. Nor is the passive voice invariably a marker of the scientific register only. It can also be observed in many forms of public announcement, especially in short orders and notices – "Trespassers will be prosecuted", "Litter must be placed in the bins", etc. Whenever a high degree of impersonality is required, the passive voice is likely to be used. Another example that will be easily recognised is the frequent use, in the language of political debate, of metaphors such as tightening the belt, ensuring fair slices of the cake for all, keeping a finger on the pulse of the nation, guiding the ship of state, and so on. Certain markers are clearly identified as being indicative of the register of religious language – the use of archaic forms such as 'thee', 'unto', 'brethren', the use of an introductory phrase of address before proceeding with a statement ("Dearly beloved, we are gathered here . . ."); the prefixing of that phrase with the word 'O' when directly addressing God; the use of the Capital letter in written language for the pronoun 'He' in referring to God; and many more.

Examples of such linguistic registers connected with occupations and activities could be multiplied over and over again – advertising language with its marked use of heavily modified nominal groups and its fondness for certain adjectives such as 'fresh', 'new', 'warm'; the language of medical consultation with its "How are we today?" where 'we' means 'you'; the language of newspapers with its frequent use of noun-adjectives and its strong reliance on words such as 'horror' and 'terror'. It is quite impossible to categorise all such registers and to list the appropriate markers. Only two points need be made; first, the markers are never entirely exclusive to one register, but can be common to many, each register being distinctive because of its unique combination of markers; and secondly, it should be noticed that the markers are a combination of grammatical and lexical features.

One major distinction that should be made is that between spoken and written English. The two modes of expression do not exist in entirely watertight compartments, but there are some features which tend to be characteristic of one mode rather than of the other. Written English on the whole has a higher degree of formality and complexity than spoken. For example, the contracted forms of verbs ('couldn't', 'didn't', 'can't') which are normal in speech, are not normal in the written mode unless by deliberate choice for a special reason. Again, the written language employs complex sentences, often with a considerable number of dependent clauses, to an extent rarely found in spoken English. Spoken English often employs incomplete sentences and verbless sentences, whereas in written English this is a comparatively rare feature. Sentences beginning with 'and', 'but' and 'so' are much more frequent in speech than in writing. There is also the question of the vocabulary used. In speech we tend to use a relatively simple vocabulary, whereas in writing we often use longer, rarer, more 'learned' words, which are well known to us but do not normally find their way into our speech. There are also numberless phrases which are markedly colloquial and therefore appropriate to speech but not to writing, expressions such as 'couldn't care less', 'completely fed up', 'bored to tears'. Many such expressions are more than merely colloquial, and could be described by the more extreme term 'slang'. It is not the presence or absence of all these linguistic features which characterises either spoken or written English; rather it is the *degree* to which such features are present.

Many registers, of course, are marked by a vocabulary which necessarily belongs to the particular activity concerned. Almost every activity has its own technical terms, and it is only to be expected that a medical text-book will include words that would not be expected in, for example, a weekly musical newspaper. Such words will be perfectly comprehensible to the initiated, but will usually be quite outside the experience of the layman. In its correct situation, technical language is not merely appropriate; it is essential. The same language would be highly inappropriate if transferred to a different situation – if a surgeon were to order meat from his butcher in the language of the operating theatre, or if a lawyer were to write to his fiancee in the words reserved for articles in the legal journals.

In addition to such necessary technical terms, there are in virtually all walks of life examples of expressions and grammatical forms which are common to the particular activity but largely unknown to the outsider. Teachers, pop groups, dentists, miners, footballers – all have their own 'language' when they are among their own kind, and often this language forms part of the mystique of the profession. As with technical terms, it is perfectly appropriate in the correct situation, but again it appears incongruous either when used by its practitioners in a different situation or when used by outsiders in an attempt to appear knowledgable.

As has been said, all language must be considered correct if it is appropriate. The only language which jars is language which is inappropriate – a light conversation conducted in 'literary' language, a formal essay written in the looser manner of colloquial speech, a discussion on general subjects into which one of the participants introduces his own professional technical vocabulary. One common example of inappropriateness is the use of what is called 'jargon'. This occurs when people engaged in some activity mistakenly imagine that there is a need in that activity for its own peculiar language, whereas in fact no such need exists. The most common jargons are probably those of business correspondence (though this is fast disappearing) and 'official' or 'Civil Service' English.

Another example of inappropriateness is often found in the use of slang. Of its nature, slang tends to be ephemeral. At one moment a certain expression is 'in' and can be used in suitable situations without causing any comment. But quite suddenly it may be replaced by a new 'in' word, and the use of the original thereafter will strike the listener as incongruous. At one time the slang of R.A.F. aircrew enjoyed a wide currency, but not often now do we hear 'wizard prang', 'ditched in the drink', or 'he bought it'. In the field of pop culture, we will make little impression if we still talk of hep-cats, scat singers and zoot suits, yet not many years ago these words were part of the essential vocabulary of all who wished to be 'in the know'.

Wherever we have any kind of 'in' language – a language which, in its grammar and lexis, belongs to a clearly recognisable group – we have what is called a dialect. This term is used mostly in a geographical sense, but it can be applied equally to professions, leisure activities, social classes, or anything that binds together one group of people to the exclusion of all others. In the geographical sense, the term is very familiar. We all know of differences between the language of Glasgow and that of Aberdeen, between the language of south-eastern England and that of the southern states of the USA. These differences are not merely differences of pronunciation. Each dialect contains a great deal of vocabulary which is its own, and even the grammar can show many differences. There is no one regional dialect which is correct; all exist, and all are of equal value. We do use the term 'Standard English', which means the conventions of language adopted, especially in writing, by all educated users of English. But Standard English is not peculiar to any one region: it is universal. Even habitual users of Standard English have their own regional dialect which they use when it is appropriate, and they all, like everyone else, have many other dialects also. For example, a Glasgow dentist who, among other things, is an enthusiastic golfer, has a family, and is an elder of his church, will have at his command several dialects – Standard English, the Glasgow regional dialect, his private family language, the language of the golf course and that of the club-house, the language of religion, and no doubt many others. We all have this variety of language at our command, and switch with ease from one to the other according to the company we are in. The efficient exponent of English is not the one who invariably uses Standard English: he is the one who has a wide range of dialects at his command and who knows always which dialect is the appropriate one to use. The inefficient exponent of English is the one whose range of dialects is so limited that he is unable on some occasions to use the forms which are expected of him.

Punctuation

When we speak our language, we all manage to indicate the structure of our remarks by punctuating them with pauses of varying lengths and with various inflexions of the voice, raising it at some points and lowering it at others. Everyone knows how to do this, and everyone does it correctly without being taught. In writing, these vocal devices are not available to us, and to replace them a system of visible marks of punctuation has gradually developed. The conventions of punctuation are not absolute rules of right and wrong, but over many years the system has achieved general acceptance, and nowadays it is possible to lay down conventions which can be departed from only to a limited extent. The ability to use the conventions of punctuation in the accepted way is important, and frequent failure to use at least the most important of these conventions correctly must be seen as a sign of incompetence in the handling of the written language. Efficient punctuation is, of course, only one factor in assessing the competence of a writer, but its importance should not be overlooked. A great deal of tolerance may be exercised regarding slackness in the use of punctuation marks in the middle of a sentence. Some writers use a great many commas, whereas others use very few. A comma in the wrong place will jar, but the omission of a comma where one might be expected is rarely considered serious. It is essential, however, to be able to indicate correctly that a sentence has come to its end. It is the failure to do this which is an indication of incompetence. For this reason, the various forms of 'end punctuation' will be treated first.

The full stop: This mark is used to indicate the end of any complete utterance that is not a question or an exclamation. It represents the long pause and the downward inflexion of the voice used by a speaker for the same purpose. Every speaker knows when his sentence is finished and acts accordingly, yet many seem unable to realise this when they set down their sentences in writing. The greatest possible care must be taken over this, since the full stop is certainly the fundamental mark of punctuation. Speech should be the guide here: if in speech we would drop the voice and stop, then in writing we should use a full stop. A certain looseness in this matter, however, may occasionally be tolerated. A style of narrative writing has developed in modern times in which, in order to convey speed and terseness, a succession of short sentences, all of similar structure, may appear loosely punctuated by commas rather than by full stops. This is a device sometimes known as the 'comma splice'. No examples will be given, because it is a most dangerous model, and not one to be imitated. If it is done deliberately for a definite purpose it may just be tolerable. If, however, as is very common, it is not really a deliberate comma splice but sheer error, then it deserves to be very heavily penalised in any examination.

The question mark: This is another example of end punctuation, and its omission must be regarded as serious. It is used in the same way as the full stop, except that it occurs only at the end of a direct question in which the actual words of the question are used. Thus we write, "Where are you going to?", but "He asked me where I was going." There are certain apparent questions which are in fact merely conventional phrases, and in such cases ("How do you do.") the question mark may be replaced by a full stop.

The exclamation mark: This is a mark which indicates the end of an exclamation, not a statement, question or command:

What a beautiful day!
How horrible!

It should not normally be used in commands, except perhaps to indicate particular urgency in the command. We would normally write "Hurry up.", but "Hurry up!" sometimes occurs to convey vehemence. Occasionally we find exclamation marks doubled or even trebled – "Hurry up!!!" – but this is usually a mark of very juvenile writing. As a general rule, the exclamation mark should be used sparingly, and only for a clearly defined purpose. If in doubt, the full stop should be preferred.

Internal punctuation of a sentence is often very helpful to the reader, and its efficient use is an indication of skill on the part of the writer, but its omission or infrequent use is often acceptable. Only the most common uses of internal punctuation will now be described.

The comma: The comma is always an indication of a brief pause in speech. The reason for the pause may be one of many, but always the implication is that there is more of the sentence to follow. In some situations the comma is necessary; sometimes it is not strictly necessary but convention dictates that we use it; in other cases its use is nowadays considered optional, and there is a tendency for it to be omitted.

The comma is necessary sometimes to avoid ambiguity and ensure precise definition. For example:

> This song is being sung in response to many requests by Tom Jones.

Here there is uncertainty as to whether the song is being sung by Tom Jones or the requests were made by him. The uncertainty is removed by the addition of commas:

> This song is being sung, in response to many requests, by Tom Jones.

One case deserves special mention here, the case of defining and non-defining clauses (sometimes called restrictive and non-restrictive):

> The house which has a red roof costs £25 000
> The house, which has a red roof, costs £25 000.

These two sentences are very different. In the first case, several houses are in existence, and one in particular is being singled out – the house which has a red roof. The others, presumably, cost more or less than £25 000. The clause 'which has a red roof' is a defining or restrictive clause, and is not marked off by commas. In the second case, only one house is under consideration. What we are talking of is 'the house', the only one, and it costs £25 000. The fact that it has a red roof is additional information, not necessary to the definition of what we are talking about. This time the clause is a non-defining or non-restrictive clause, and it is separated from the rest of the sentence by commas. Another way of putting it is that in the case of the non-defining clause the subject of the sentence is 'The house', whereas in the defining clause the subject is 'The house which has a red roof'. Here the expression 'which has a red roof' is not a true adjectival clause but a rank-shifted clause operating as a group, and is the item 'q' in the structure of the nominal group whose headword is 'house'.

The comma more often is not strictly necessary to convey meaning, but convention demands that it be used. One of its most common uses of this type is to separate different items in a list:

Tea, sugar, butter, bread and milk.
She was young, graceful, charming and intelligent.

Here, a comma between the second last item and 'and' may be used and often is.

Another common use is to indicate items in apposition:

Mr. Docherty, the team manager, has named a pool of sixteen players.
My cousin, George Brown, is very keen on politics.

A similar use is to indicate any interruption in the flow of the sentence:

His excuse, it seemed to me, was very feeble.
My father, however, decided to accept it.

Often the decision whether or not to use a comma is a matter of taste rather than rule. This occurs especially in any long or complex sentence, where the writer may feel that the use of commas will help the reader by indicating how the sentence breaks into its component parts:

When we consider the many problems that now beset us, and when we reflect upon the simplicity of former days, it is no wonder that, from time to time, we ask ourselves where it is all going to end.

Here, all the commas are acceptable, yet it would be equally acceptable to omit any or all of them. The current tendency is to reduce rather than increase the number of commas used, and certainly for the inexperienced writer the best advice would be not to use a comma if there seems to be any doubt about the matter.

The semi-colon: Like the comma, the semi-colon indicates a pause in the course of a sentence. The difference is simply one of intensity. The semi-colon always indicates a more emphatic pause than the comma, but it is not so final as the full stop. There is always something more to be said before the statement is complete. A good example of its use for this emphatic purpose is to be found in 'Julius Caesar':

> "As Caesar loved me, I weep for him; as he was fortunate, I rejoice at it; as he was valiant, I honour him; but as he was ambitious, I slew him."

Here we have a series of grammatically independent statements, but to separate them by full stops would be to lose their close interconnection and to use commas would be to lose the special emphasis that is to be placed on the final "I slew him." In order to grasp the value of the semi-colon – and indeed of the full stop and the comma – it is only necessary to read Shakespeare's sentence aloud three times, first as it appears above, then using full stops in place of the semi-colons, and finally substituting commas. The differences will be noticed at once.

There is one situation in which the semi-colon is particularly valuable: to separate items in a list when the items are lengthy and themselves include commas. For example:

> Among those present were Arthur Ford, a distinguished Past President of the Society; Donald McRae, who has recently returned after a period of two years in New York; John Gilmartin, our efficient Secretary; and Martin Murray, making a welcome reappearance after his recent serious illness.

Obviously the semi-colon is a very useful mark of punctuation, but nowadays it tends to be reserved for formal rather than informal writing. It is important to be able to recognise why a writer has used it and what is its effect, but for the inexperienced writer the best advice is to use it sparingly and only when there is no doubt that it is the best mark to use in the situation.

The colon: The colon indicates a pause even stronger than that indicated by the semi-colon. It usually introduces some item which is absolutely necessary for the completion of the sense of the sentence. The words after the colon must in some way fulfil the expectation aroused by the words before it. For example:

> There are only two possible explanations for your conduct: either you are very stupid, or you are very impertinent.

It can occasionally appear even when there is no necessary completion to follow if it is to indicate a very strong pause, particularly if some sharp contrast is being expressed. For example:

> Those who can, do: those who can't, teach.

Again however, this is something to be observed and understood when it is encountered rather than something which the inexperienced writer should try to imitate.

There remains, of course, perhaps the most common use of the colon, to introduce a quotation. Here it is often accompanied by a dash (:-), but the current tendency is to use the colon alone:

> This is a sentiment which has been admirably expressed in the well-known lines by Burns:
>
> > "The rank is but the guinea's stamp,
> > The man's the gowd for a' that."

The dash, and brackets: These two punctuation devices are very similar in function but not always interchangeable. Their chief use is to mark off some serious interruption in the flow of a sentence, something which is in effect a separate sentence inserted into a statement being made. For example:

> I met Tommy in the club last night – he usually goes there on Mondays – and he was telling me a strange story.
>
> There was one man there (I recognised his face but I don't know his name) who seemed to feel very strongly about the subject.

In these two examples the dashes and brackets are interchangeable. If, however, the interruption consists of more than one sentence, brackets rather than dashes are used.

> I met Tommy in the club last night. (He usually goes there on Mondays. That is the night when his wife entertains her girl friends.) He was telling me a strange story.

A single dash is often used as a strong comma in places where a semi-colon or perhaps even a colon could also occur:

> All of these people have the same function – they exist to serve the public.

This usage is becoming more and more widespread nowadays, and it is perfectly acceptable, but it should be used sparingly. It is very handy, but it does not allow the precision which is possible if we are confident in the use of the comma, the semi-colon and the colon.

Inverted commas: These are used before and after the actual words used by a speaker in direct speech, the words of a quotation, and the titles of books, musical works, films, ships, etc. For example:

> "Give it to me," he said.
> Hamlet's dilemma, "To be or not to be", is one which many people have faced.
> George Orwell's "Animal Farm" is a great political satire.

The inverted commas can be either single or double. This is simply a matter of taste, though normally in handwriting double inverted commas are used whereas in printing there is a tendency for single to be preferred. Some adopt the practice of using single inverted commas for very short, even one-word, items and double for anything longer. In both printing and handwriting it is customary to use both single and double when, for example, a title or quotation occurs within an item which is already enclosed in inverted commas.

> "Last night," said James, "I saw 'Hamlet' on television."

In addition to end punctuation and internal punctuation, there are also some marks which are not true punctuation marks at all but are essential features of the words themselves. Such devices may be referred to as word punctuation.

The hyphen: The hyphen is a short dash which is used when two or more words are joined together to form one compound word – a ready-made suit, a walking-stick, out-of-date ideas, hero-worship, etc. In many cases the new compound thus formed becomes so familiar that eventually it appears as one word without the hyphen. Thus there are many words which are in a transitional stage, when some writers use the hyphen and others do not – folklore, taxpayer, flyover, for example.

The apostrophe: The apostrophe has two separate functions:

(i) to denote the contraction of a word by the omission of a letter or letters, and
(ii) to indicate possession

The former function is fairly simple. In conversation we normally contract the negative form of many verbs. Thus,

do not   – don't
could not   – couldn't

33

Other contracted forms of the verb are equally familiar.

I am   – I'm
they are   – they're
we have   – we've

Wherever there is an omission of letters for any reason, they are replaced by the apostrophe:

huntin', shootin' and fishin'
a cup o' tea
fish 'n' chips
four o'clock

The only note of caution required is that you must ensure that the apostrophe appears in the correct place – the place where the omission has occurred. Thus,

shouldn't   *not*   should'nt
hadn't   *not*   had'nt

The second function of the apostrophe – to denote possession – ought to be equally simple, but for some reason it is here that mistakes most frequently occur. The first thing to remember is that the apostrophe indicating possession is found *in nouns only*, not in pronouns. Thus you may expect to see *child's, Tom's, men's, or brother's*, but not *her's, your's* or *it's*. (The form *it's* does occur, but only as the contraction of *it is*.) Secondly, the possessive apostrophe in nouns is normally used for living creatures only, not inanimate objects. Thus,

the blade of the knife   *not*   the knife's blade
the girders of the bridge   *not*   the bridge's girders

Now we come to the method of forming the possessive of the noun. It is best to consider first only the case of a noun which is in the singular, since it is really very simple. You take the noun as it stands, add an apostrophe, and after the apostrophe you add the letter s. Thus.

dog   – the dog's bone
child   – the child's scooter
man   – the man's hat
fox   – the fox's lair
ass   – the ass's ears

34

witch	– the witch's cauldron
James	– St. James's park.

Notice that no alteration in spelling is involved, no insertion of the letter 'e' in some cases, no dropping of any final letter – simply add the apostrophe and 's' to the existing form. You should notice, however, that where conformity to the rule would result in a pronunciation difficulty the final 's' is not added. Thus we say (and write) *Moses' brother* rather than *Moses's brother*.

The formation of the possessive of a noun in the plural is slightly more complicated. Once again, you start with the normal plural form of the noun – dogs, children, men, foxes, asses, etc. Next you examine the ending of the word. If it does not end in 's', then you proceed as for the singular noun – simply add an apostrophe and 's':

children	– the children's toys
men	– the men's overalls
women	– the women's cloakroom

If, however the noun ends in 's' in the plural form, it is treated differently – an apostrophe is added but no additional 's'. Thus,

dogs	– the dogs' bones
asses	– the asses' ears
ladies	– the ladies' waiting-room
witches	– the witches' cauldron

The only difficulty here is that many words alter their spelling slightly when they form their plural – asses, ladies, witches, etc. This is, however, a spelling matter. It has nothing to do with the formation of the possessive. Provided that you know the plural form of the noun, you should be able to transform it into the possessive.

When the apostrophe is encountered, it is always easy to recognise why it has been used. Many people, however, have difficulty in using it for themselves, and often their policy is to add an apostrophe before every final 's', often with ludicrous results. For all who experience this difficulty the best advice is to go to the other extreme and drop the apostrophe entirely. An apostrophe in the wrong place is a positive error, whereas the omission of an apostrophe in no way hinders understanding and is more and more coming to be accepted as a legitimate practice.

The abbreviation mark: Many words appear regularly in an abbreviated form, and this is indicated by the use of a mark identical with the full stop at the end of the word. It is not, of course, a stop of any kind, but is frequently referred to as a full stop. Examples of such abbreviated forms are well known: Rev. James Morgan, St. James's Park, M.A., B.Sc., e.g., etc.

Whenever an abbreviated form is used the punctuation mark may be employed. There are some cases, however, where it is optional. There are many well-known sets of initial letters which by sheer familiarity have tended to lose their abbreviation mark: UNO, BBC, USA, TUC, etc.

Another case is that of a word whose abbreviated form includes the final letter of the full word. Here, many writers prefer to omit the abbreviation mark, though others retain it. Thus the abbreviated forms of Mister, Doctor and Street can be either Mr, Dr and St or Mr., Dr., and St. The choice is open, but as in all matters of punctuation modern practice tends to favour omission wherever a choice occurs.

Capital letters: The use of the capital letter is clearly defined, and causes few difficulties. It occurs chiefly as follows:

(a) The first word of a sentence.

(b) The first word inside a new set of inverted commas. The capital letter is not used, however, when a sentence of direct speech is resumed after a brief interruption: "I think," said Zebedee, "that it is time for bed."

(c) All words in titles except for very short words such as conjunctions, prepositions, etc.:
Brave New World
Of Mice and Men
The Turn of the Screw.

(d) Proper nouns and their adjectives, races and religions, days and months, large organisations, names for God including pronouns, etc.:
Scotland, Scottish
The Negro race (but a negro)
Protestantism
Sunday, January
British Steel Corporation
God, He, His Son

(e) The personal pronoun 'I'

(f) In most poetry, the first word on each line. This convention, however, is broken frequently nowadays.

Many other occasions exist when the capital letter is used, but these are the principal cases. They present no difficulty in recognition, but some students are not always sure when to use capitals themselves, and as a result they tend to use them too liberally. As usual, the best advice is to be conservative – to use capitals when certain but if in doubt to leave them out.

Typographical devices: In speech, if a word requires special emphasis this is achieved by the use of an emphatic tone of voice. In writing, such emphasis can be indicated in several ways. In handwriting and typing, the word to be emphasised can be underlined or written in block capitals. In printing, italics can be used, and the printer also has at his disposal many different kinds of type to indicate the word which requires to be stressed. Suppose, for example, in an examination there is the instruction "Candidates should attempt any three of the five questions." The word 'three' is obviously very important here, and it can be emphasised in several ways:

Underlining	–	<u>three</u>
Block Capitals	–	THREE
Bold type	–	**three**
Italics	–	*three*

A Note on Spelling

The ability to spell words correctly is of some importance. Certainly the consistently weak speller is at a disadvantage, since many who read his writings will form an impression of incompetence which may not be deserved. However, its importance must not be exaggerated. It is more important to know a word and to be able to use it effectively than to know how to spell it. No one should ever refrain from using the word he thinks to be the best in the context and substitute a less effective word simply because he knows how to spell the one and not the other. It is only when spelling errors are so frequent and so gross that they hinder the communication of ideas that this weakness should be considered serious. In the Higher English examination, weakness in spelling will be considered and will probably be penalised, but only to the extent of a few marks over the whole paper, and never to the extent of failing a candidate who otherwise would have passed.

Unfortunately, little help can be given here to the weak speller. The only sound way to learn to spell correctly is to read and observe. This is a slow process which begins at the age of five and continues throughout our lives. What makes some people better spellers than others is simply the fact that when they read they notice little things and are gradually able to absorb them, until they recognise correct spelling because it looks right and incorrect spelling because it looks wrong. Many attempts have been made over the centuries to devise efficient ways of teaching and learning spelling, but these are necessarily very laborious processes and there is little evidence that they can ever completely succeed in their objective, unless the poor speller is caught at an early age. However, for those who are really keen to improve their spelling, there is one well tried method which, while it will not transform a bad speller into a good speller overnight, will if persisted in produce results in the long term.

It is not a matter of memorising spelling rules (there are too many of them and too many exceptions) or of memorising spelling lists. It involves instead concentrating on the particular word that is causing difficulty and observing closely how it is made up: its individual syllables, recognisable common clusters of letters, peculiarities such as silent letters, unusual combinations etc. Once the word has been thoroughly studied, it should be memorised, not in parrot fashion but bearing in mind all the features observed. The next step is to cover up the word and try writing it for yourself. You then check for correctness and if necessary repeat the process. In cases of serious and persistent difficulty, it sometimes helps at the study stage to trace the outline of the word with the finger. The important thing is to concentrate on those words which cause you difficulty rather than contemplate an assault on the entire English language. The only spelling list of any value is one which is tailored to the needs of the individual student. In the rush of preparation for Higher English it may not be feasible to devote much time to this necessarily lengthy process. In the long term, however, the method outlined here should produce results.

COMPOSITION

The Examination Paper

Paper I of the Higher English examination sets out to test skill in the writing of continuous prose. This it does in two ways, by means of two questions, both of which must be attempted. In Question A there is a wide choice of subjects, but in Question B no choice is allowed. The whole paper carries 50 marks, with usually 35 for Question A and 15 for Question B. The time allowed is 1 hour 40 minutes.

The two questions are very different in character. In Question A, the candidate must supply from his own knowledge or imagination material which is relevant to the question asked and express this material in a form and style appropriate to the subject. In Question B, however, the material is supplied to him and his task is to select what is relevant to the instructions given, to organise the material in a logical order, and to express it in a formal style and in a tone appropriate to the task involved. Thus Question A offers an opportunity for writing which is personal and original, reflecting the character and interests of the writer, whereas in Question B nothing of the writer's personality must appear.

In the course of this chapter, the two questions will be treated separately. It should be realised, however, that a great deal of what is said about Question A will apply equally to Question B, especially everything which deals with the planning of the work, the structure of the paragraphs, and sentence structure. Timing of the work and the length of the composition are equally important in both questions, as is the need for care in spelling, punctuation and handwriting. Most of these matters will be dealt with under Question A, and the section on Question B will deal only with those matters which are peculiar to that question.

Question A – Choice of Topic

In Question A a very wide range of topics is offered in the hope that every candidate will find something which appeals to him and which is within the range of his knowledge and ability. It is important to take advantage of this wide selection and choose wisely.

One of the most important factors in assessing a composition is the extent to which it reveals the writer's liveliness and individuality. Composition should never be a dry, dutiful exercise in conformity to a set of rules. It should be an enjoyable experience, and the finished work should reflect the enjoyment the writer has found in his writing. It follows, therefore, that the subject chosen must be one which appeals to the writer and one on which he has knowledge or firm opinions. If he writes with enthusiasm for his subject then what he writes can never be dull. It may have many technical faults, but it will have the chief virtue of all good writing, interesting subject matter. In order to achieve this the candidate should consider the topics offered with three factors in mind.

The first of these is that a subject should be chosen which is within the candidate's knowledge or experience. This can be demonstrated very easily if we consider two examples taken from the 1979 paper:

> "It is my firm intention, some time during the second half of my life, to do something about the wonky handle on the sitting room door."

> Write about all those things which you mean to tackle in the future but which you know you may never get around to doing.

Here the candidate must have a genuine sense of things in his life that require to be done and a rueful feeling that somehow they are never going to be achieved. Clearly this can be done only by someone who fits this description.

> "a haphazard mixture of love, exploitation, and destruction"

> Using the above quotation as a basis for your composition, write about the relationship between people and animals.

This topic should be chosen only by those who have thought about this relationship and can back their opinions with some factual knowledge of the subject. If you have no such knowledge to offer, you should seek some other topic.

Even when a fictional subject is chosen – a short story, for example – the characters and situations must be within the writer's experience or at least very close to it. The whole story, of course, will not be a mere recounting of something which has happened to the writer, but he must have some first-hand knowledge and understanding of the kind of people he chooses to write about and the events that take place. To write about an American soldier in Vietnam, for example, or about a secret agent operating in East Germany, will almost inevitably result in mere imitation of other writers – probably writers who themselves were not writing from experience. It is surely better to choose a more familiar setting and the sort of people who are frequently encountered in real life.

The second consideration is closely related to the first. Not only should we know about the subject chosen; we should also have feelings about it. Genuineness of opinion is very important. Again, two examples will illustrate this.

> "There are only two things I cannot abide. One is insularity, and the other is foreigners."

> About which issue (political, economic, religious or social) have you had difficulty making up your mind one way or the other? Explain clearly in your composition the nature of your dilemma, and at some point indicate your present stance.

Here the candidate must have a genuine issue of this kind in mind, must know what his present stance is, and must still be uncertain as to the resolution of his dilemma. Clearly this can be done only by someone who is genuinely in this situation. If you have not experienced such a dilemma, you simply cannot answer the question. It would be possible, of course, to search your mind for some views which you might assume for the occasion, but in this case you would be unlikely to convey any enthusiasm for the subject.

> "The feeling that most of us have for the place of our birth is a kind of fond contempt."

> Write about your birthplace in such a way as to bring out its attractions and its less endearing qualities. (You may treat "birthplace" on a local, or regional, or national level.)

This topic should be chosen only by those who actually have feelings about their birthplace and whose feelings meet the two requirements of the rubric: fondness and contempt. If you have no such feelings, then you must seek some other topic.

The third factor which must be considered in choosing a topic to write about is the type of writing that is being asked for. The register required must be within your knowledge and capabilities. Many topics are offered which call for a special kind of writing – a magazine article, a talk, a letter, a short story, etc. An example from the 1978 paper will demonstrate this.

You have been asked to deliver a speech to an audience of your contemporaries in which you argue for the motion "Television does not just transmit; it transforms". You will consider the effect that television has had on yourself, your contemporaries, and on society generally.

Again, you must know the subject, you must have opinions on it, but you must also be familiar with the form required. This is a *talk* to *a group of contemporaries*, and the composition must show the markers appropriate to such a situation. You must decide on the degree of informality and collo-quialism expected, you must be aware of such public-speaking techniques as the use of the rhetorical question, and you must remember the use of such terms of address – "Ladies and gentlemen," perhaps – as are common in talks.

These then are the three vital questions:
Do I know about the subject? Do I have clear views about it?
Can I write in the manner required?
All three are important, and only if all three can be answered positively will it be likely that a lively and interesting composition will result.

Relevance

Having chosen a topic which appeals to you, you must now ensure that you keep within the limits imposed by the instructions. Sometimes even enthusiasm can be dangerous, for it may lead an unwary writer into matters connected with the subject but irrelevant to the precise demands of the question. Irrelevance in a composition will result in some penalty being imposed. The extent of the penalty will depend on the degree of irrelevance displayed. Three different types of irrelevance can occur, and these are penalised in different ways.

The most serious type of irrelevance is the composition which has absolutely no connection with the topic chosen. Such a composition really deserves no marks at all, but in fact it will be given some credit for the skill with which it is written. No matter how skilfully it is written, however, it can never be given a pass mark. Fortunately such compositions are rare, and presumably no intelligent candidate will run such a risk.

The least serious case is that of the composition which deals with the topic but occasionally strays off into matters not strictly relevant to it. Provided that the topic is adequately covered, this additional material can usually be ignored, or at worst penalised to the extent of two or three marks. Nevertheless, although any penalty will be small, there is a danger that this loss of marks may bring the total mark for the whole examination down from the A category to B, from B to C, or worst of all from C to failure. Obviously some care should be taken, therefore, not to wander off the point.

The type of irrelevance which causes most difficulty lies between these two. This is found in a composition which deals with the topic required but fails to meet the precise demands laid down in the wording of the question. For this, direct penalties will be imposed. When the composition is to be marked out of 35, a typical penalty for such irrelevance would be to mark it out of 30, or in more serious cases 25. To incur such a penalty is to court disaster. It is still possible for such a composition to secure a pass mark, but obviously it would have to be of very good quality to do so. Unfortunately this type of irrelevance is very widespread, and often this accounts for the disappointing results achieved by fairly competent candidates. Sometimes candidates incur this penalty simply by carelessness in reading the question. In their excitement they fail to notice that it is a talk they have to compose, or that they have to write "in light-hearted vein", or that what is required is description rather than narration. The greatest care must therefore be taken to read the question very closely and to ensure that its terms are met. Very often, however, this type of irrelevance is brought about not by carelessness or excitement but by the deliberate use by the candidate of material he has prepared beforehand. There is no doubt that many people are guilty of reproducing in the examination a piece of writing that they have used on a previous occasion. In the course of their practice writing they may have managed to write well on one or two topics and they decide to store these up for later use. In the examination they find a topic which is on the same lines as one of their prepared essays, and they blatantly reproduce their treasured work. Almost invariably in such cases the composition produced fails to meet the precise demands of the question and a penalty has to be imposed. Such candidates – all too many of them – deserve no sympathy. They are guilty of a dishonest attempt to sidetrack the purpose of the examination, and they usually fail in their attempt. It cannot be too strongly stressed that no candidate should ever enter this examination determined to make use of a prepared essay.

Some examples of the penalties which might be imposed for this type of irrelevance can be shown in a few of the topics set in 1978 and 1979.

"Whenever I look inside myself I am afraid."
Consider the dangers of analysing yourself **and** the dangers of failing to do so.

A composition which considers only the dangers of self analysis and ignores the dangers of its omission would warrant being marked out of 30.

> The following are extracts from publishers' "blurbs" on four different books. Write what would be an appropriate extract from **one** of these books in which you **describe** a scene or incident.
>
> (*N.B. A short story is not acceptable here.*)

Absence of description (which is prescribed in heavy black type), or the writing of a self-contained short story rather than an extract (which is specifically barred in italics) would certainly be penalised.

> Write a short story which concludes with **one** of the following:

This time a short story *is* asked for, and failure to produce one would result in a reduced mark out of 30.

In the example already quoted of the speech on the effects of television, examiners will be as generous as possible in deciding what might conceivably be a speech, but any composition which is clearly *not* a speech will be penalised.

These are only a few examples of what can occur and how it might be treated by an examiner. They should be studied closely in order to realise the justice of the penalties imposed. A worthwhile exercise would then be to pick out all the other topics in the 1979 paper and any other papers available, and in each case to consider carefully what pitfalls would have to be avoided. In the examination itself, of course, such a close scrutiny (at least of the topic finally selected) is absolutely essential.

Separate mention should be made of one type of subject, the title which consists of a single word or a short phrase, with no other instruction (What would happen if . . .; once bitten . . .; Beauty). Here the candidate is free to write as he pleases – a short story, a reflective essay, or anything which can be related to the title. He must however, ensure that the word or phrase of the title is not merely incidental to the composition: it must be central to it.

Timing and Length

Paper I is worth 50 marks, and the time allowed is 100 minutes – in other words, two minutes for each mark. Thus a 35-mark composition might occupy 70 minutes, a 30-mark composition 60 minutes. In fact, however, it is probably wiser to decide on approximately 60 minutes for Question A regardless of the number of marks allocated, leaving 40 minutes for Question B.

In the hour available a great deal has to be done, and there is no time to waste. In view of the importance of making a wise choice of subject, probably as much as five minutes will be required before a final decision is reached. A further five minutes will be required at the end for a close scrutiny of what you have written and the improvement of any obvious weaknesses. This leaves only 50 minutes for planning the work and actually composing it. The importance of planning and a method of doing so will be explained later. You will certainly need at least 10 minutes for this important activity. Thus only about 40 minutes can be spent in the actual task of composing and writing. Thus a sensible allocation of time would be:

5 minutes	–	choosing
10 minutes	–	planning
40 minutes	–	composing
5 minutes	–	revising

These times can be varied slightly, but it is essential to complete the whole process within the time allowed, since question B still remains to be done and it poses special time-consuming problems.

Many candidates discover to their cost on the day of the examination that it can be very difficult to complete this whole process in one hour. The wise candidate, however, knows well in advance exactly how much he can do and how he must set about it. This knowledge can be achieved only by practice. In the course of many months of preparation, many compositions should be attempted, and from the very beginning the student should work by the clock, so that in the end skilful timing of the work will have become almost second nature. Even in practice compositions a definite limit of one hour should be set, at the end of which the composition must be finished. At first you may find yourself forced to crowd into the last few minutes some of the most important points you want to make, thus destroying the overall effect of the composition. As a result of this you will learn not to ramble on about unimportant matters but to allow for adequate treatment of all the aspects of the topic you want to cover, especially the ending.

It is impossible to lay down exactly how long a one-hour composition should be. The syllabus until recently laid down a length of 400 words or more, but in recent years has made no prescription beyond advising that one hour should be spent on the composition. In practice a 400 word composition tends to be rather slight in content, and anything between 500 and 600 words is the normal. Such a figure should not be thought of as a target to be reached. The best approach is that of time: the correct length is the amount that can be achieved in one hour's hard work. If you plan your composition thoroughly and write it thoughtfully, in accordance with the methods which will be described in the rest of this chapter, you may find at first that you can produce only about 200 words in the time. It would be tempting then to sacrifice thoughtfulness and thoroughness for sheer bulk, but this would be foolish. The composition must first of all be written along sound lines, and once the method has become familiar you will find that quantity will be increased along with quality. The time of one hour should be the constant factor. At the end of each composition, count the number of words, and in time you should find yourself comfortably producing about 500 words each time. This figure need only be approximate of course. In the examination itself there is no need to count the number of words used. To do so would be to use up valuable time for no reason. No rigid limits are laid down by the examiners and they certainly do not expect any candidate to state how many words he has used. The composition will be assessed on its quality, not its length. This applies equally to Question B. If any number of words is stated in the question it is intended only as an approximate guide, not as a prescription. The only point in the whole of the English examination where length is a serious matter is in the summary in Paper II, and this will be dealt with at the appropriate point in the next chapter.

Planning the Composition

The best way to ensure that your composition is relevant, that it is of the required length, and that it makes its points effectively is to draw up an outline of its structure before you begin. A clear structure is the chief distinguishing feature of a good composition. Without careful planning, the usual result is looseness and disorder, with important points omitted or badly placed, and a rambling style which often fails to lead to a well-rounded conclusion. It may safely be said that a good composition simply cannot be written without planning of some kind. It may be possible for some gifted writers to plan their work mentally but most people need to set down on paper the plan which they intend to follow. A good method of doing this is as follows:

(a) Compose a brief title for the whole composition.
(b) Compose sub-titles, as short as possible, for each paragraph.
(c) Under the paragraph titles add a few notes to indicate the ground which is to be covered.

The general title should be short, simple and clear. There is no need to think up a clever title, something amusing or 'poetic'. What is required, in fact, is in effect a summary, in two or three words, of the whole composition. Having thought about the subject chosen, and having decided what is expected, you then try to express this in one short phrase which will indicate how you are going to deal with the subject.

Next you must consider in more detail what you want to say and decide on a series of sub-titles, each of which will indicate the subject-matter of one paragraph. The nature of this plan will depend, of course, on the type of composition being written. A composition which presents an expression of opinion will require a very different plan from one which is purely descriptive. In all cases, however, the plan should follow some order – perhaps chronological order for narrative writing, place order for descriptive writing, or order of importance (ascending or descending) for a series of opinions.

The main title and sub-titles – if they are adhered to – will ensure that the whole composition will have a recognisable structure and that it will make its point effectively. The final stage of the planning is to decide on how each paragraph will be developed. Under each paragraph title, a few notes should be written indicating what will be said in the paragraph. These notes should be as brief as possible, jottings rather than lengthy phrases or sentences. You must avoid allowing your plan to develop into a rough draft of the actual composition. At this stage you should be concerned only with the subject-matter, not the way in which it will be expressed.

At this stage it would be as well to illustrate from one of the topics already mentioned how a useful plan might be drawn up.

> "It is my firm intention, some time during the second half of my life, to do something about the wonky handle on the sitting room door."
>
> Write about all those things which you mean to tackle in the future but which you know you may never get around to doing.
>
> Title: The Things I Shall Never Do

Having chosen this title, you are now almost forced to be relevant. By keeping the title firmly in mind you will ensure that you deal with both aspects of the subject: your awareness of the tasks that ought to be done, and your realisation that you will never actually do them.

Next the paragraph structure must be determined. This could be done in many different ways. One such method would be to write an opening paragraph introducing the topic, followed by, say, three paragraphs each dealing with one of the tasks you have chosen, and then a final paragraph rounding the whole thing off. Thus the paragraph sub-titles might be the following:

1. Introduction
2. Books and Records
3. Garden
4. Car Maintenance
5. Conclusion.

This may not be the best paragraph plan possible, but at least it will guarantee that the finished composition will have some shape to it.

The next step is to consider each of the sub-titles, and under each make a few notes on particular points to be mentioned. These should, of course, be no more than jottings which will be expanded when the composition is being written.

The final plan then, might be as follows:

The Things I Shall Never Do

1. Introduction: Need to change haphazard way of life.
2. Books and Records: Storage and cataloguing.
3. Garden: From wilderness to ordered layout.
4. Car Maintenance: From helplessness to skill.
5. Conclusion: "The best laid schemes . . ."

All that remains is to ensure that the composition follows this paragraph outline, and the result will be a composition that is relevant, substantial in amount, and having a clear structure. The actual writing of the composition will be dealt with in later sections.

Here is another example, this time topic (j) in the 1979 paper:

"a haphazard mixture of love, exploitation, and destruction"

Using the above quotation as a basis for your composition, write about the relationship between people and animals.

People and Animals

1. Introduction: Love, exploitation and destruction overlapping.
2. Love: Domestic pets, farm animals, animals in the wild.
3. Exploitation: Work, sport, factory farming.
4. Destruction: Seal culling, whale hunting, disturbance of ecology.
5. Conclusion: One-way relationship in Man's favour.

A method of planning such as this should be adopted every time you write a practice composition and in the examination itself. In addition, it would be a valuable exercise to compose plans for as many topics as possible in the Past Papers, even if you do not intend to write the composition in full. In this way, you will develop skill and speed, and you will learn a great deal about the vital subject of relevance.

The Structure of the Paragraph

Once the paragraph plan is completed, the task of actually composing begins. To do this effectively, it is best to think in terms of paragraphs as the basic units, each paragraph being formed from the material included under each sub-title in the plan.

A new paragraph always begins on a new line, and the first word is usually indented – that is, instead of beginning at the margin it is moved slightly to the right, usually about one inch in handwriting. Paragraphs can be of any length, short or long, depending on the subject-matter. A new paragraph is not started purely on the grounds of length; it begins when one topic is completed and a new topic is to be started. The problem of when to begin a new paragraph is solved, of course, if you work to a plan: you simply begin the new paragraph when you have finished all you want to say under one sub-title. By working in this way you will ensure that each paragraph has unity, in that everything in it will be concerned with the same topic.

The nature of the topic of the paragraph should be immediately clear to the reader. Normally this can be achieved by the use of a sentence at or near the beginning of the paragraph which is a brief statement of the topic which is to follow. This usually is known as the *Topic Sentence*. A common, and effective, paragraph structure consists of a short, clear topic sentence followed by a series of sentences all amplifying the topic, with the whole thing rounded off by a final short sentence which is, in effect, a re-statement of the topic in another form. A good example of this type of paragraph structure is the following paragraph which occurs in "Captain Sharkey", a short story by Sir Arthur Conan Doyle, in which he is describing the ways of certain pirates:

"They were the more to be dreaded because they had none of that discipline and restraint which made their predecessors, the Buccaneers, both formidable and respectable. These Ishmaels of the sea rendered an account to no man, and treated their prisoners according to the drunken whim of the moment. Flashes of grotesque generosity alternated with longer stretches of inconceivable ferocity, and the skipper who fell into their hands might find himself dismissed with his cargo, after serving as boon companion in some hideous debauch, or might sit at his cabin table with his own nose and his lips served up with pepper and salt in front of him. It took a stout seaman in those days to ply his calling in the Caribbean Gulf.''

Here the topic is clearly stated in the opening sentence: the menace of these pirates. The paragraph goes on to give examples of their unpredictable ferocity. Then the final sentence in effect re-states the topic: that these men were dangerous.

It is not always necessary to compose paragraphs in exactly this way. Indeed, it is not even always possible. Nevertheless for an inexperienced writer it is a good model to follow as often as possible until some degree of expertise is reached. Certainly the topic sentence at least should always be used. Remember that it should be fairly short, it should be a clear statement of the topic, and should occur at the beginning of the paragraph. This should be a feature of all the compositions you write, but for additional training it would perhaps be wise to practise it more frequently. It has already been suggested that you should draw up paragraph plans even for some subjects on which you do not intend to write a full composition. You could carry this a stage further by composing also a topic sentence for each paragraph. In all of your reading also you should observe the topic sentence in use.

Paragraph Linkage

As we have seen, a composition should have a clear structure of paragraphs, and each paragraph should itself have a structure that gives it a unity. The paragraphs of a composition do not exist in isolation, however; they are all part of the one structure and must be suitably linked together to show their relationship to each other and to the whole work. If not, what is produced is not one composition but a disconnected series of separate little essays.

The best place to introduce the link between paragraphs is the opening sentence of the new paragraph. This opening sentence should be a clear statement of the topic to be discussed, but it should also include some item which establishes its connection with what has gone before. It is not advisable to use the last sentence of a paragraph as the introduction to the new one, because this would damage the unity of that paragraph by the introduction of something entirely new.

The linking device which is used at the beginning of a paragraph is often quite unobtrusive. Very often it consists of no more than a word or phrase which might be thought of as the key idea of the previous paragraph. In the case of the paragraph which you are now reading, for example, the opening sentence makes a statement about "the linking device". Since the whole of the previous paragraph dealt with the connecting link between paragraphs, the use of this expression serves as the link in this case. Often it is possible to make the connection even stronger by the use of 'this' instead of 'the' – "This linking device", for example. 'This' serves a double function here: it acts as the determiner of the modifier of the nominal group which is the subject of the sentence, and it also points back to the topic of the previous paragraph.

The passage set in the Interpretation paper in 1978 shows an example of this linking device in action. The first paragraph describes certain aspects of suburban life showing that suburban dwellers have certain good qualities which are not fully developed. The second paragraph, which goes on to argue that, given these characteristics, suburban society is incapable of producing or supporting major drama, opens with:

> "These negative virtues are not the source of profound drama or literature ..."

Here, not only do we have the key phrase "negative virtues", which sums up the characteristics described in paragraph 1, but also the link has been strengthened by the use of "these".

As well as this fairly unobtrusive method of linking paragraphs, it is possible also to use one of many words or phrases which exist for the specific purpose of linkage. There are very many of these, all very familiar: moreover, in addition, however, on the other hand, secondly, another reason, although, etc. These can easily be observed in any reading that you do. They are, of course, indispensable items in writing, but they should be used cautiously. The repeated use of the same or a similar device throughout a composition can give it a very dull, pedestrian quality. For example, in the composition "things I shall never do", you should avoid the monotony of opening successive paragraphs with

> "The first task that I would like to carry out ..."
>
> "Another task ..."
>
> "A third task ..."

Some effort must be made to introduce variety of linkage. For example, instead of "A third task ...", it would be better to link this paragraph to all that has gone before with something like:

> "All the examples of wishful thinking I have described so far have been concerned with domestic matters: now I shall turn to one long-cherished ambition which would benefit me in all my travels through life."

Similarly, you must avoid excessive use of "In the first place", "Secondly", "Thirdly" in case you should find yourself beginning a paragraph with something ridiculous like "Thirteenthly".

Some form of paragraph linkage, then, should be introduced wherever possible. At first this should be a very deliberate process, but eventually it will come naturally. As well as doing this in all the compositions you write, you could add this to the outline compositions already recommended. These would now take the form of a title and plan with the topic sentence of each paragraph, including in each case except the first some linking expression.

Sentence Structure

Just as the unit within the whole composition is the paragraph, so the unit within the paragraph is the sentence, and the task of writing a paragraph is the task of writing in complete sentences. The ability to do this competently is, of course, absolutely vital, and certainly no one will pass in Higher English who cannot write in sentences. The nature of the sentence was fully covered in Chapter One in the sections on grammar and punctuation, and anyone who has difficulty in this matter should work hard on these sections. As was said before, it is strange that everybody has this ability in speech, yet many fail when it comes to writing. The solution to the problem lies, of course, in constant practice, both in reading and writing.

The essential thing about the sentence is its completeness. It can be long or short, simple or complex. It can even consist of only one word. But in all cases the whole thing is complete. The reader should never be left waiting for what is to come next, nor should he find himself reading several sentences loosely strung together with commas as if they were all the one sentence – the so-called comma splice. When the utterance has come to a stop, there should be a stop – a full stop, question mark or exclamation mark as the case may be.

To write a good composition, however, it is not enough merely to write in sentences which are technically 'correct'. This may be enough to secure a pass, but little more. A good composition must be lively and interesting not only in subject-matter but also in style, and this liveliness is achieved partly through the use of a variety of sentence structures.

The simplest way to produce a varied style is by variation of sentence length. A paragraph which consists entirely of very short sentences can be very successful if it is attempting to convey a flat monotony (a technique employed very effectively by Ernest Hemingway in 'A Farewell to Arms'), but for most normal purposes short sentences should be used more sparingly. They can be particularly effective as topic sentences, and equally so when they are used to round off a paragraph with a re-statement of the topic. In between, however, some longer sentences should be employed. Allied to this matter of length is the degree of complexity of structures used. The simple, one-statement sentence can be used, but it may be followed by a double sentence linked by 'and' or 'but', and then perhaps by a complex sentence containing a main clause with several other clauses dependent on it, before another simple sentence is used. Again, the pattern of the word order can be varied. Instead of composing every sentence in the standard SPCA order, there can be occasional devia-tions, such as bringing the item A to the beginning, especially if this item is a complete adverbial clause or a participle phrase. Finally, not every sentence need be a statement. An occasional question or exclamation can be very effective in producing variety, provided they are not used to excess.

These, then are four ways in which variety can be introduced into a paragraph:

Long	/ short
Simple	/ complex
SPCA	/ ASPC, etc.
Statement	/ question / command.

All four can be observed whenever you read any competent writing, and all four should be consciously adopted into your own writing. To end this section, there follows a paragraph from 'The House with the Green Shutters' by George Douglas. If you study it carefully you will observe a clear topic sentence, a development of the topic, and a final re-statement of the topic. You will also observe the variety that is produced by the employment of all four methods that have been described:

"Both in appearance and position the house was a worthy coun-terpart of its owner. It was a substantial two-storey dwelling, planted firm and gawcey on a little natural terrace that projected a considerable distance into the Square. At the foot of the steep little bank shelving to the terrace ran a stone wall, of no great height, and the iron railings it uplifted were no higher than the sward within. Thus the whole house was bare to the view from the ground up, nothing in front to screen its admirable qualities. From each corner, behind, flanking walls went out to the right and left, and hid the yard and the granaries. In front of these walls the dwelling seemed to thrust itself out for notice. It took the eye of a stranger the moment he entered the Square – 'Whose place is that?' was his natural question. A house that challenges regard in that way should have a gallant bravery in its look; if its aspect be mean, its assertive position but directs the eye to its infirmities. There is something pathetic about a tall, cold, barn-like house set high upon a brae; it cannot hide its naked shame; it thrusts its ugliness dumbly on your notice, a manifest blotch upon the world, a place for the winds to whistle round. But Gourlay's house was worthy its commanding station. A little dour and blunt in the outlines like Gourlay himself, it drew and satisfied your eye as he did."

Lexical Choice

We have dealt with the whole composition, the paragraphs which go to make it up, and the sentences which are the units of the paragraph. Now we come to the choice of words to be used within each sentence. Here there are two considerations, effectiveness and appropriateness. An effective word is one which successfully conveys the writer's intentions: an appropriate word is one suited to the context in which it is used.

Normally we can easily find a word which says what we want to say with reasonable effectiveness. In successful writing, however, the word so easily found is often changed for one which does its work even more effectively, and the good writer is one whose lexical choice is very deliberate and not hap-hazard. Everyone is familiar, for example, with those words which are used so widely to cover so many different shades of meaning that they have become entirely hackneyed and ineffective – words like 'get', 'nice', 'terrible', 'awful', etc. It would be wrong to say that these words should not be used in writing, but certainly they should not be used unless by deliberate choice. Almost always a better word can be found with a little thought. Again, there are many words which are not hackneyed but which do not of themselves carry all the meaning that may be required. A verb like 'walked', for example, has a clear meaning, but there are many different kinds of walking, and these can be conveyed by the choice of words more effective in their contexts, words like 'strode', 'strolled', 'marched', 'sauntered', 'tiptoed'. They all mean 'walked', but with very different shades of meaning. Sometimes the word chosen may be very effective, but because it requires to be used several times in a short passage variety must be introduced by substituting a slightly different word on some of these occasions. There is also the possibility of increasing the effectiveness of your writing by occasionally departing from the literal use of words and using figurative language, such as simile and metaphor, in order to create a clear visual image in the reader's mind of what you are describing.

Effective lexical choice can be observed in the work of any good writer. Here is a paragraph taken from "A High Wind in Jamaica" by Richard Hughes:

> "For the children, those first few days at sea had flashed by like a kind of prolonged circus. There is no machine invented for sober purposes so well adapted also to play as the rigging of a ship: and the kindly captain, as Mrs. Thornton had divined, was willing to give them a lot of freedom. First came the climbing of a few rungs of the ratlines in a sailor's charge: higher each time, till John attained a gingerly touching of the yard: then hugged it, then straddled it. Soon, running up the ratlines and prancing on the yard (as if it were a mere table-top) had no further thrill for John or Emily either. (To go out on the yard was not allowed)."

A great deal could be said about the words chosen here, but only a few points will be made. Notice, for example, the two similes used ("like a kind of prolonged circus" and "as if it were a mere table-top"). Then consider why the word 'sober' was chosen to describe 'purposes'. Most important of all, notice the progression contained in the verbs used in the latter part – attained, hugged, straddled, running, prancing. Other words in the paragraph would repay some close thought. A similar approach could be made to passages in all of your reading in order to discover the great care that good writers take in order to achieve effectiveness in their lexical choice.

Appropriateness of lexical choice is an equally important consideration. First of all, the register chosen must be the correct one for the situation. In formal writing, there should be none of the highly colloquial vocabulary that is appropriate to informal conversation. A speech or an article should carry some of the markers of these forms. All this was dealt with in the section on Register in Chapter One.

There is also the question of a simple vocabulary as opposed to a more ornate style. This is often a matter of taste rather than of rule. Generally speaking, a simple vocabulary tends to be effective, but there are many occasions when a more 'learned' vocabulary is required to achieve fine shades of meaning. Both types of vocabulary are, of course, acceptable, but the choice of a florid style in an ordinary situation or of an over-simple style in a situation which calls for something more adventurous would be inappropriate. The former fault is very common among fairly talented candidates in Higher English when they attempt purely descriptive writing. It occurs also on any occasion when a writer is trying to impress with the extent of his vocabulary. Since this is a weakness in writing, it is difficult to illustrate it from the work of any reputable author, but it is often used deliberately by some authors as a form of ridicule of such a 'learned' style when it is used inappropriately. A good example of this deliberate over-writing occurs in the language of Wilkins Micawber, a character in Charles Dickens's 'David Copperfield'. In the following passage, Mr. Micawber is offering to show young David Copperfield the way to the house in which he is to have his lodgings:

> "Under the impression", said Mr. Micawber, "that your peregrinations in this metropolis have not as yet been extensive, and that you might have some difficulty in penetrating the arcana of the Modern Babylon in the direction of the City Road, – in short," said Mr. Micawber, in another burst of confidence, "that you might lose yourself – I shall be happy to call this evening, and instal you in the knowledge of the nearest way."

One feature of this 'fine writing' which often occurs in descriptive writing is the excessive use of the technique of ascribing to the world of nature human feelings which are meant to reflect the mood of the character involved in the piece of writing (a literary technique sometimes known as the 'pathetic fallacy'). Thus, if a mood of loneliness and grief is to be conveyed, the skies will be weeping and the call of the gulls will be a cry of anguish. The sea will retreat from the shore leaving the rocks to mourn their new-found isolation. Even the pallid lighthouse will stare out to sea as if bereft of all warm companionship. Used in moderation this can be effective enough, but when used to excess, as it often is by young and inexperienced writers, it can become inappropriate and even ridiculous. Again, illustration of this fault is difficult. It would be possible to quote some examples from the work of school pupils, but this would be unfair on such people who are trying their best to rise above a uniformly drab and colourless style and have not yet learned the restraint that must go with it. Perhaps it is enough, however, merely to have drawn attention to the pathetic fallacy and to the need to employ it in moderation.

Different Types of Composition

Most of what has been said so far applies to composition of all kinds. Certain types of composition, however, have particular features that deserve some special attention. A few such points now follow.

Description – Be careful to avoid excessive narration of events. A certain narrative element may be present in order to give some framework to the composition, but the bulk of the composition should be descriptive. The aim should be to make the reader feel that he is present at the scene, or can visualise the person, or can savour the excitement of the occasion. The planning of such a composition can be quite difficult. Unless some logical order is thought of, there is a danger that the piece will be entirely formless. It is for this reason that some kind of narrative framework may be helpful. In descriptive writing, good lexical choice is particularly important, especially the use of effective figurative language and the avoidance of excessively 'fine' writing overladen with the 'pathetic fallacy'. Some element of descriptive writing will feature in many different types of composition. For examples of purely descriptive composition, see 1979 (f) and 1978 (f).

Narrative writing – Again, an element of narration will occur in many compositions, such as description and personal memories. The normal order for narration is of course chronological. Anything which presents an account of events can be described as narration, but the form of narrative that presents most attraction and most problems for the Higher English candidate is the short story (see 1979 (e) and 1978 (f)). This is a very popular item in every examination paper, but unfortunately it is usually very badly done, since it is a particularly difficult type of writing to achieve.

A short story is far more than a series of events presented in chronological order. It is a story with a point to it. Some years ago candidates were invited to write a short story set in a supermarket. Almost without exception they produced a tale of a poor but respectable widow subjected to sudden temptation, the act of shoplifting, her detection (or avoidance of detection), remorse and final forgiveness. This is narrative writing all right, but it is not a short story, chiefly because of its ending. It ends because the episode is finished, but nothing has happened to give the reader any sense of surprise, pleasure, sadness, or understanding of a human character. The first step in planning a short story is in fact to decide on its ending in order to ensure that such an effect is produced.

The early part of a good short story is often given over to establishing character – usually only one character, almost certainly no more than two, since within its limits the short story is unable to deal successfully with any more. There is no need to give every last biographical detail, but at least the reader should know what sort of man he is dealing with and what situation he is in, happy or miserable, active or inactive, lonely or surrounded by friends. This character will probably be a perfectly normal person drawn from first-hand or nearly first-hand experience – a 17 year old schoolgirl, an ordinary husband and father, a bed-ridden pensioner –

rather than something esoteric like a New York gangster, a Russian spy, or a wartime fighter pilot. Only when the character is fully established should events be introduced. These events should be kept to a minimum, and at all costs you should avoid over-sensational events. It is distressing to read so frequently a 500-word story – which is after all very short – crammed with theft, violence, jail breaks, explosions, kidnapping, espionage, and a host of other happenings which would be more than enough for a full-length novel and which could not conceivably be within or even close to the experience of the writer. In fact, perhaps only one event will occur, and it may be no more sensational than an offer of a helping hand across the road or a surprisingly uncharitable remark. Such an event would normally be of little significance, but happening as it does to *this* person, in *this* situation, it is of such importance that he is in some way a changed man: his eyes are opened, his world collapses around him, the clouds hanging over him disappear, or some such radical change. If the story has been well told, there is no need for the consequences of this event to be spelled out for the reader. He knows the character, he appreciates what has happened and he can picture for himself the consequences.

To achieve all of this with such limited material and in such a short space is no mean achievement, and it should not be attempted by anyone who is not familiar with the short story form and has not developed some skill in writing it. In order to learn more about the short story, the only course is to embark on an extensive programme of short story reading. There are countless good collections of short stories in existence, and there should be no difficulty in finding them. Such a course of reading will give great pleasure and will do nothing but good, but it is by no means certain to make a good writer of short stories. The form involves a degree of artistry and discipline which is not found in most Higher English candidates, who would be better employed in finding an easier type of composition to write.

If, despite all this, you do attempt to write short stories, there is a further difficulty that must be mentioned, the difficulty of writing good dialogue. Dialogue figures prominently in most fictional writing, and it is not easy to produce. The words used must give the impression of being naturalistic, but in fact will be far removed from the way people actually speak in real situations, as might be transcribed from a tape recorder. Then there is the difficulty of the linking narrative – "said James", "he replied", "Mary answered", etc. It takes a skilled hand to do this without excessive repetition of the same formula. Even a simple thing like the punctuation of dialogue can be difficult for the unskilled. Yet the use of dialogue is virtually an essential feature of every good short story. The only advice possible, then, is to acquire this skill by observation of other writers and by practice, but not to employ it in short story writing in the examination unless you are satisfied that you really can do it. Finally it must be said that some candidates do acquire this skill, and some short stories are produced which are quite brilliant.

Expression of opinion – The most frequent type of composition is one in which the candidate is asked to present his views on a topic of controversy. Usually at least three such subjects appear in any paper. Examples can be seen in 1979 (a), (b) and (h) and in 1978 (e), (i) and (k). Occasionally the instructions may ask for a balanced discussion of both sides of the question, but normally the candidate is expected to take one side or the other and argue his case strongly.

If a strong expression of opinion is to emerge, it is essential that you make up your mind on the question at the planning stage, before you start to write. Your argument should not be a careful and fair weighing-up of both sides, ending with a reasoned 'verdict'. Such a treatment may produce a well planned and well reasoned argument, but it will lack the spark of individuality which distinguishes the good essay from the merely competent. Your opinion should be firmly held, and it should be made clear from the very first sentence. The opening paragraph should leave the reader in no doubt as to the nature of the controversy and your attitude to it. Successive paragraphs will then deal with several arguments supporting your view. Near the end you should, perhaps, deal briefly with the opposite viewpoint, attempting to show the weaknesses of this side, but should then finish strongly with a firm re-statement of the view you originally expressed, coloured but not altered by the arguments raised in the course of the composition. Thus a basic plan to cover all such compositions might be:

(a) Statement of attitude
(b) Argument 1
(c) Argument 2
(d) Argument 3
(e) Refutation of opposite viewpoint
(f) Re-statement of attitude.

In such a case, the first and last paragraphs should be as vehement as possible, so that there is no doubt as to the view you wish to put forward, and particular attention should be paid to effective lexical choice. For the remaining paragraphs, perhaps the most important factor will be clear paragraph linkage designed to show that each argument is only one stage in the entire process.

The reflective essay – This is a type of writing similar to the expression of opinion in that it presents something of the writer's mind and personality, but it differs in that it is not necessarily intended to be argumentative and persuasive. Examples of this type of composition can be found in 1979 (c), (d), (g) and (i) and in 1978 (d), (g) and (h). The subjects can range from matters of the moment – an unfortunate encounter with modern technology – to the realms of abstract thought – What would happen if ... In all cases, what is expected is a revelation of the writer's personality as he adopts his own attitude to the subject and treats it in his own personal way. When it is well done, this can be a most attractive type of writing, and it is in this field that most candidates do their best work.

There are as many ways of tackling such a composition as there are candidates, and it would be wrong to recommend any one way. The importance of planning, however, cannot be too strongly stressed. Without a clear plan, firmly adhered to, such a composition can become mere ramblings which fail to reach anywhere and fail to make any impact on the reader.

A brief word might be given again to one-word and short-phrase titles such as "Beauty" and "Isn't it incredible . . .". These can be treated as reflective essays, of course, and probably should be, but in the absence of any other instructions there is nothing to prevent their being treated in any other way, such as the short story, provided that the word of the title does not merely figure somewhere in the composition but is central to it. Sadly, it is very often the case that the given word or phrase is used solely as a quick means of entry to a weak short story which has nothing to do with the implications of the title.

Special registers – It has already been pointed out that particular care is required when any special register is to be adopted, such as the article, commentary, extract from novel, talk, letter or diary. In addition to all the usual problems of planning, paragraph structure, paragraph linkage, sentence structure and lexical choice there is the extra need to write in the register appropriate to these special cases, with sufficient markers of the chosen register to indicate that it is being consciously adopted. Examples of this type of composition occur in 1979 (f) and in 1978 (c) and (j).

As was said before, this type of composition should not be attempted unless the register is familiar to you. Given that it is, then what you have to do is to think yourself into the situation, imagining the audience before you, the hall in which you are speaking, the readers of your article or letter, its lay-out on the page, the television programme through which your voice as commentator will speak, etc. You are inventing a fictitious situation, but what you write must be as close to reality as possible.

The letter form requires a special word here. The Higher English examination does not normally seek to test accuracy of letter lay-out in such matters as address, salutation and subscription. All that is normally required is something like a letter to a newspaper, in which the only lay-out necessary is "Dear Sir" at the beginning and "Yours faithfully" followed by your signature below it at the end. It is assumed here that the normal conventions of letter lay-out are already known to candidates. Apart from this, no special treatment of the letter is required. Like any other kind of writing, it should be planned in paragraphs, the paragraphs should be linked, and the sentences should be competently composed in effective and appropriate words. No other technique is involved.

A brief word should be said also on the extract from a novel or other full-length book. The task set varies from year to year (usually descriptive writing or creation of character) and candidates should be careful to offer the type of writing that the question requires. The other matter of importance to remember is that this is to be an extract, not a complete work.

Question B

Question B is different in several respects from Question A, although it remains basically the same, a test of skill in continuous writing. The essential differences are that in Question B the candidate does not choose his own subject-matter but is supplied with the material he is to use, and he is not free to select an appropriate style but is told to adopt a formal, impersonal style, and to write in a tone appropriate to the material and to the instructions given.

There is a great deal of common ground between the two questions, however. The main stages in the process of composition are exactly the same. These are what was covered in the sections headed Planning the Composition, The Structure of the Paragraph, Paragraph Linkage, Sentence Structure and Lexical Choice. It will be assumed throughout this section that these previous sections have been thoroughly mastered.

The different stages that must be gone through in Question B can be listed as follows:

    (a)   Careful interpretation of the instructions given.
    (b)   Careful interpretation of the material given.

(c) Selection of all that is relevant to the instructions and rejection of the irrelevant.

(d) Organisation of the relevant material in a logical paragraph structure in such a way as to bring out those matters which are of chief importance and to subordinate those matters which are of minor importance.

(e) Selection of the appropriate tone.

(f) Expression of the relevant material in good, continuous prose in standard English.

Interpretation of instructions – The instructions given must be very carefully read in order to ensure that the precise task set is fulfilled. The need for this can best be illustrated from the instructions given in the 1979 paper:

> As the pupil representative on Dunmalcolm Grammar School's Leisure and Recreation Committee, you have been asked to write for the school magazine an article on Achinver, a cottage which has been gifted to your school by Colonel W. L. Kent, estate owner and distinguished former pupil.
>
> The committee has instructed you (a) to inform pupils, staff, and parents of the gift to the school; (b) to give details of the cottage and its whereabouts; (c) to outline the committee's plans for the cottage; and (d) to demonstrate how its advantages as an outdoor centre outweigh its disadvantages.
>
> From the notes and sketch you have made on a visit to Achinver and from the material provided by the committee, select what is relevant, rearrange it as you think best, and then write your article in 250–300 words of formal, continuous prose.

It should be noted that you have been set a fourfold task here, and you must ensure that you cover all four parts. First you must inform your readers of the gift, probably quite briefly. Next you must describe the cottage and its location, selecting those details which you think are of most importance and will be of greatest interest. Thirdly you will explain how the cottage is to be renovated and used by the school. Finally you are to acknowledge certain disadvantages (which you must identify for yourself from the material) but go on to show that the advantages (which again you must identify) outweigh these disadvantages. Note that you are not asked to make any decisions. These have all been made already by the committee; you have merely to report them. The suggested length of your article (250–300 words) is intended as a rough guide, not a prescription, and you should not waste time counting the number of words.

A similar inspection of the 1978 paper will reveal that in this case you are to write a leaflet for local distribution in which you will do three things: inform people of an impending threat to their way of life; make clear why you and your associates are opposed to the proposal; and indicate what action you intend to take. Again, the length suggested is intended to be only approximate.

Whatever instructions may appear, you must interpret them in such a way as to be clear in your mind as to who is presenting the statement, to whom it is being presented, and what is its overall purpose. These matters must then be kept in mind throughout the remaining processes.

Interpretation of material – It goes without saying that the information given must be read carefully and fully understood. There is no intention that this task of accurate interpretation should be part of the examination, and it is assumed that all the material will be readily understood by all candidates. In fact, some little difficulties of understanding may arise, so great care must be taken to reduce these to a minimum. No help can be given in this matter – you simply read and understand.

Selection of material – It may be that some of the material given is unnecessary for the overall purpose of the report that is to be presented, and if so such material should be discarded. What is irrelevant is often a matter of opinion, of course, and you will not be penalised for selecting what others might consider irrelevant provided that you integrate it properly into your text. If, however, something is left out which in the opinion of the examiners is essential, then the resulting report will be incomplete and will be penalised accordingly. Generally speaking, little if anything of the material supplied should be left out unless it is clearly irrelevant.

Organisation of material – Once all the relevant material has been selected, the next task is to put it into some logical order – in other words to compose a paragraph plan. A report of this nature will always consist of several paragraphs, each dealing with one aspect of the subject. It will never be a matter of merely reproducing the information given in the order in which it is presented to you. There will always be some re-ordering of the material, grouping pieces of connected information together, evaluating the relative importance of the different pieces of information, and presenting it all in a coherent form. In a way it is the opposite process to summarising. Once the unimportant has been discarded, what is left is not to be pared down but to be built up from its skeleton form into a complete passage.

To do this, a plan should be drawn up in the usual way. A plan for the 1979 question might be drawn up as follows:

Achinver Cottage

1. Information: gift, details, whereabouts.
2. Plans: renovation, use.
3. Advantages v. disadvantages.

For the 1978 question, the following plan might be used:

Glenvale Residents Association

1. Information: Proposed petro-chemical plant.
2. Objections to the proposals.
3. Action to be taken.

These are not the only possible plans to use, nor are they necessarily the best, but they serve to illustrate the kind of planning which must be done if the subject is to be adequately treated in a coherent manner.

The headings that are used here are, of course, merely part of the plan. They are not to be used as headings in the finished version. It may be argued that in practice many reports do make use of headings, but the instructions for this examination are clear. What is required is continuous prose, and headings should not be included. If they are, they will at best be disregarded but at worst will be positively penalised if, by using headings, the candidate has failed to make use of proper paragraph linkage, and has thus produced not one complete composition but a series of short, separate items.

Tone – One important feature of Question B is that you must decide on the tone in which the piece is to be written. The requirement of "formal continuous prose" does not mean a piece of writing which is formally "correct" but otherwise featureless. On the contrary, Question B always involves the candidate in a piece of extended rôle-playing in which he must be clear as to who he is supposed to be, what he is writing, for what purpose he is writing it, and who is his intended reader. By being totally aware of these four points, you will ensure that the tone is appropriate both to the material itself and to the nature of the task you have been set.

Often the question itself makes it quite clear what the tone is to be. 1979, for example, prescribes an article for a school magazine, and this dictates the tone. 1978 included "forcefully summarise the association's objections to the plant". In 1977, an educational correspondent of a good quality national newspaper was to write an article for parents on the use of calculators in schools, and among other things was to "make recommendations". 1976 required the easily recognisable tone of a radio news bulletin. 1975 called for a "firm but courteous letter". These are just a few recent examples of how the question can guide you along the right lines.

Expression – With all of the planning completed, the final task is to compose the report itself. As has been said, this is to be done in a formal, impersonal style. This style can best be described in a negative way. It is simply the absence of anything which is a marker of colloquial writing, dialect, personal usage, or any kind of 'in-group' expression. In other words, it is neutral English, not a form of language which has its own characteristic jargon. The term 'impersonal' need not be taken too literally. It does not mean a heavy reliance on passive constructions such as "It is to be assumed that . . ." or the impersonal pronoun "one". There must be no expression of the candidate's personality, but in the Achinver article, for example, it would be legitimate to say "We have decided . . ." rather than "It has been decided . . ."

There is no rule against using the words given in the notes, but to do so would not always be advisable. These original notes – since they *are* notes – will almost certainly be written in an informal register in places. Many examples of this can be found in the 1979 question:

> pretty desperate, gobble up wood, ugh!, bring wellies.

It is very unlikely that the pupil who made these notes during his visit to the cottage would use any of these expressions when writing his formal article.

Another feature of the notes that must be watched is the use of numbers. There may be occasions when the notes make use of figures whereas in formal writing these numbers would probably be written as words – 4 miles, for example. This is not to say, of course, that all numbers should be written in words. Normal practice should be followed, giving large numbers, prices, quantities etc. in figures but others in words. Thus we have 2 000 men, but four miles; £2 500 rather than two thousand five hundred pounds.

Often there will be parts of the notes which require expansion, especially when symbols and punctuation marks are used. Examples are numerous:

> 90% of heat; ugh!; (1946–1952); small parties (a Mini-busful); (many undesirable?); GLENVALE: (pop. 693)

What is produced, then, should be formally correct in style but slanted in tone to fit its particular purpose, and written always in complete sentences. Beyond that, all the normal rules of good composition apply – well-linked paragraphs, good and varied sentence structure, effective and appropriate lexical choice – resulting in a short composition which reads well. With all this preparation and writing required, it is essential that you allow adequate time for the whole process. As was said before, Question A should be completed in one hour, leaving a very necessary 40 minutes for the adequate treatment of Question B.

INTERPRETATION AND LANGUAGE

The Examination Paper

Paper II of the Higher English examination sets out to test skill in understanding a piece of English and knowledge of language usage. Once again, two questions are set, both of which must be attempted. In each case there is a passage of prose with a series of questions on it. The whole paper carries 50 marks, with usually 40 for Question A and 10 for Question B. The division of marks may vary very slightly from year to year and indeed there is provision in the syllabus for the shorter passage to appear as Question A and the longer as Question B, although so far this has never happened. The time allowed is 1 hour 30 minutes, which represents about 75 minutes for Question A and 15 minutes for Question B.

The two questions are rather different in character. Question A follows more or less traditional lines, and is concerned chiefly with the candidate's understanding of the full meaning of the passage. Question B deals with different varieties of language, and is not so much concerned with what is said as with how it is said – not the meaning alone, but how the meaning is achieved.

As in the other papers, there is a great deal to be done in the time available, and many candidates find themselves unable to finish the paper. This is something which you must not allow to happen. A great deal of time is often wasted by candidates who write far more than the question demands or deserves, and this is something which can easily be avoided with a little thought. For example, many candidates seem to believe that all questions must be answered in complete sentences, but this is not always the case. Several questions in each paper state quite clearly that all that is required is to set down a particular phrase from the passage, or to quote four different words, or to give two examples. There is no point, for example, in the 1979 paper, in writing.

(d) (ii)   The question is being asked by the young Israelis.

when all that is required is

(d) (ii)   The young Israelis.

Similarly it is pointless to write (1978):

(c)   The definition which is most appropriate in the case of "the comfortable humours" is "temperament or disposition of mind"

when all that is required is

(c)   "temperament or disposition of mind".

Even for questions which clearly require to be answered in complete sentences, a great deal of time can be wasted by writing too much. After each question, the number of marks attached to it is shown in brackets. This is intended as a guide to the candidate as to how much he should write. A two-mark question will probably deserve no more than a sentence or two, whereas a four-mark question will probably require a fairly lengthy answer to deal with it adequately. Obviously, then, the marks allocated should be noticed before the question is answered.

Another reason for failure to complete the paper is mental exhaustion. Question A consists of a lengthy passage of some difficulty, and many of the questions are quite searching. After an hour and a quarter of this, some candidates find it difficult to make the mental adjustment to the new question based on a totally new passage, and in the remaining 15 minutes their minds go so blank that they are barely able to take in the meaning of the passage, never mind attempt to answer the questions. For all who, in practice attempts, experience this difficulty there is a lot to be said for answering Question B first of all, when the mind is fresh, and then going on to Question A. In the later stages, when exhaustion may be setting in, at least the passage will be familiar, and there will no longer be the difficulty of turning the mind to something completely new. If this course is adopted, however, you must make sure that you spend no more than 15 to 20 minutes on Question B, since there is a great deal to be done in Question A.

Question A

General Remarks – The syllabus describes the prose passage that will be set in Question A as being one "of moderate difficulty". In effect what this means is that it should be within the range of understanding of most intelligent, educated readers, but it will demand a close scrutiny before its entire meaning can be grasped. This close scrutiny will be required not so much because of any serious difficulties of vocabulary as because of a fair degree of complexity in the thought that runs through the passage. The degree of difficulty to be expected can be seen simply by reading through the passages which have been set in previous years.

The questions set on this passage are designed to test how well the candidate has understood what he has read. The skill that is being tested however, is not a skill in answering interpretation questions; it is a skill in understanding the English language as demonstrated in this particular passage. Interpretation is not an end in itself, like skilful piano playing or skilful typing; it is a means of assessing competence in the understanding and use of the language. Training for such a test, then, cannot be based on a set of interpretation exercises. The true training for this question is all the experience of reading and writing that has been accumulated since childhood. The candidate who is well prepared for the Composition and Literature papers will be competent in reading with understanding and writing with effectiveness. Such a candidate should be able to take Paper II in his stride.

It is not quite as easy as that, of course. Although it is not possible to undergo a successful course of training in interpretation in isolation from the other aspects of English, nevertheless some practice is essential in order to understand the format of the paper, the degree of difficulty of the questions, and the problems of completing everything in the time allowed. It is these matters with which the present chapter is concerned.

The syllabus lists the areas of competence to be tested as follows:

the meaning of words, phrases and sentences
the inter-relation of ideas
the summarising of ideas
the appropriateness of language
grammatical structure and usage
the conventions of written English.

Not all of these areas are necessarily covered in any one year. In practice, the questions are divided into four sections, with the first three items listed above normally being tested in Sections 1, 2 and 3, and the last three items (or a selection from them) being covered in Section 4. In recent years, however, the distinctions between the various sections have been becoming rather blurred, and this is a tendency which will probably continue. Indeed there are many who believe that the sectionalised format is an artificial practice which should be discontinued altogether.

Although the questions are divided into four sections, these are not to be thought of as watertight compartments, each to be treated separately

69

from the rest, and to be covered in any order. There often is, in fact, a natural progression in the sections, and they should be dealt with in the order in which they are asked. Successful completion of the first section, on meanings, makes it easier to deal with Section 2, which is concerned with the understanding of rather longer pieces of the text. When this has been completed, there should be a sound general understanding of the whole passage, which is then tested in Section 3, the summary. By now there should be almost total understanding of the passage, and this should help when it comes to dealing with the linguistic and stylistic questions posed in Section 4. It is almost impossible, therefore, to justify any departure from the order in which the questions are presented. The examiners are trying to be helpful in presenting them in this way, and it is foolish to reject the help that they offer.

One more general point must now be dealt with before proceeding to the individual sections. In the instructions given in the examination, the phrase "as far as possible in your own words" is printed in bold type. This is a very important instruction and it must be observed. It does not apply, of course, to questions in which you are told to quote an appropriate part of the passage, but in all other cases it means that you are to extract the required information from the passage but then to express it in your own words. Only in this way will the examiner know with certainty that you have actually understood what you have read. If you extract the right information from the passage but set it down in the author's words you will be given some credit for at least knowing where to find the answer, but in order to gain full marks for the question you must show that you are fully aware of what the words mean.

One example, drawn from the 1979 paper, should serve to demonstrate how this should be done. In Section 2 there occurs the question

What is the author's main point about "a people" in paragraph 1?

The first sentence of paragraph 1 reads as follows:

"It seems to me undeniable that a people has its individual character, its peculiar capacity for trust or suspicion, kindness or cruelty, energy or lassitude."

The remainder of the paragraph gives particular illustrations of this general point.

An answer which would not warrant full marks (1 in this case) might be the following:

The author's main point about "a people" in paragraph 1 is that a people has its individual character, its peculiar capacity for trust or suspicion, kindness or cruelty, energy or lassitude.

70

Here the appropriate information has been selected, and the unnecessary illustrative material has quite correctly been discarded, and so some credit is deserved. But to gain the full mark, the point must be clearly expressed in such a way as to show that it has been understood. Thus:

> The author's main point is that the character of any people is unique to that people.

This use of "your own words", then, is important throughout the paper, but especially so in the summary.

Having disposed of these preliminaries, we now come to the examination itself. The first stage, of course, is to read the passage carefully, probably once fairly quickly and then a slower, more searching inspection. Only after this do you turn to the questions, starting with Section 1.

Section 1

This section is concerned with the meaning of words, phrases and sentences in the context of the passage, although the questions are more than the simple "What is the meaning of . . ." One of the questions until recently took the form of choosing the correct answer from a set of five possibilities offered. It was phrased as follows:

> The answer to each of the questions in this section is one of the letters A, B, C, D or E. Give the answer you think is best in the context.
> (i) "abused" (line 10) means (A) ill-treated; (B) criticised; (C) mishandled; (D) attacked; (E) dismissed.

Obviously, all that the candidate had to do was to write down the appropriate letter. This was never a satisfactory question, and it is unlikely to reappear in that form. No doubt candidates will continue to be asked from time to time to distinguish between shades of meaning, but better ways of testing this will be employed. In 1978, for example, one question took the following form:

> A dictionary entry describing "humour" might include the following:
> a fluid of the animal body; temperament or disposition of mind; state of mind (*good, ill humour*); caprice; a mental quality which apprehends and delights in the ludicrous and mirthful; that which causes mirth and amusement; playful fancy.
> Which of these definitions is most appropriate in the case of "*the comfortable humours*" (line 10)?

This is much more satisfactory, since it is exactly what we all have to do in the real situation of consulting a dictionary.

The other questions in this section can occur in almost any form, and it is almost impossible to forecast the wording. The wording is significant, however, and must be closely studied. This can be illustrated from the questions set in 1978 and 1979.

> Suggest two ways in which the suburb might be said to be "parasitical" on either town or country. (2)

This is a way of asking if you know what "parasitical" means, though you are not asked to state its meaning. Instead, drawing from your own knowledge rather than from information given in the passage, you are asked to give two examples of ways in which the suburb lives off the resources of other areas.

> Choose one of the examples which the author gives of "negative virtues" (line 6) and explain clearly why it might be described as a negative virtue. (2)

Here two words are involved, and you must demonstrate that you understand them both. First, therefore, you must show that what the author has described is in fact a virtue, and then you must go on to show that it is in some way undeveloped. Two marks are offered, and to earn both you must bring out both the positive and the negative elements.

> Examine carefully the immediate context of "peculiar" (line 1) and "lassitude" (line 2). In each case, give the meaning of the word and explain how the context helps the reader to arrive at the meaning. (4)

There are two marks for each word, and in each case two tasks to be performed: first to explain what the word means for one mark, and then for the second mark to show how the context conveys the meaning. Notice that it is the *immediate* context you are told to examine; there will be no question of looking outside the sentence in which the words occur. In the case of "peculiar", the clue lies in the phrase which immediately precedes it. "Lassitude" occurs paired with "energy", and these two are part of a series of pairs, all of which are obviously opposites. It follows, therefore, that "lassitude" must be the opposite of "energy".

> What is meant by "a proposition that is popular but, on such evidence as exists, scarcely tenable"? (2)

This is a straightforward demand for meaning. But you must be careful to cover all the parts. There are in fact four: proposition, popular, evidence and tenable. Your explanation must include them all if it is to earn full marks.

Section 2

This is the section which really leads the candidate towards a full understanding of the passage. Here we are concerned not with the meaning of isolated words and phrases but with the way in which ideas are inter-related to form the thread of the writer's argument. This is probably the crucial section of Question A, and if it can be mastered then the summary which is to follow should be much easier to tackle. Normally Section 2 can be expected to carry considerably more marks than any other section.

It is difficult to say what kind of questions can be expected here, since everything will depend on the nature of the passage and the complexity of its argument. For this reason, any advice that is given can only be given in very general terms rather than on a question-by-question basis.

The first thing is to notice the number of marks offered, and take this as a guide to the length of answer expected and to the number of points that will have to be made. For example, in 1979, question (c), 2 marks are offered for an explanation of the contribution made by the last sentence of paragraph 2 to the argument of the paragraph as a whole. For 2 marks only a fairly brief answer is expected. To earn both, however, you must do more than refer merely to the last sentence. First you must establish what the argument of the paragraph has been, and then you must explain the effect of the last sentence.

In the same paper question (e) offers 4 marks for giving a description of the part of the passage (14 lines of it) in which the author gives a lengthy illustration of his whole argument by referring to the modern Israelis and how they have come to be very different from the Jews in Germany before and during the war. There is a lot of material to be considered here, and a substantial answer is required. Because there is so much material, however, it would be unrealistic to expect even very good candidates all to make the same four points and so award one mark for each. Answers are bound to vary a great deal in a question like this. What you must ensure, however, is that you give adequate cover not just to the Israelis and what has made them the people they are, but also to the German Jews and the factors which shaped their character.

Often a close scrutiny of the question will reveal that several separate things are asked for. Thus what appears, from the marks allocated, to be a question demanding a lengthy answer may turn out to be several short questions, each of which can be answered quite briefly. There is an example of this in 1977, question (e):

> Explain fully why the author thinks there are grounds for "a certain modest hope" (line 24) (4)

This is in fact the opening (or topic) sentence of the final paragraph and the remainder of the paragraph goes on to state what the author considers these grounds to be. He lists about five of them in fact. Your task is thus fairly straightforward. What you have to do is to pick out any four of them and explain what they are. This can be done quite briefly in each case.

The essential thing is to realise that in Section 2 the questions are not framed on broad, general lines. They are very precise, and must be read closely to ensure that they are fully dealt with. When that has been done and when you have noticed the allocation of marks and any possible sub-division of the question, then you proceed as indicated before: find the area of the text to which the question refers, pick out from it the author's material on which your answer is to be based, and then compose the answer using the author's material but your own words.

Section 3

Normally, you can expect Section 3 to ask for a summary of the whole passage or at least of a substantial part of it. The current tendency is for only a partial summary to be asked for. There is no guarantee that this question will always be set, but the ability to summarise is so useful in life, and is such a sound indication of competence in both understanding and expression, that it is difficult to imagine it ever being omitted. It is a question which carries a high proportion of marks, and is therefore one which must be done well. It can be a difficult thing to do well, but fortunately this is one area of the paper where training and practice can produce success. What is required is a sound method of tackling the summary, and after that as much practice as possible, using of course the past papers, but also any other material that may come to hand. What follows here is the method; the practice you must arrange for yourself.

Since the summary is worth from 6 to 10 marks, you must ensure that you have enough time available for it – something like 2 minutes per mark. If it is to be done well, a considerable amount of planning, drafting, revision and re-writing is involved, and this cannot be done hurriedly. One advantage you have, however, is the fact that before you attempt the summary you should already have a fairly sound idea of what the whole passage is about.

First of all, we should be clear as to what are the characteristics of a good summary. These may be listed as follows:

(1) It must be a fair representation of the train of thought of the original.
(2) It must contain nothing that is merely incidental to or an elaboration of that train of thought.
(3) It must contain nothing of the candidate's attitude: it is what the author says, written from his viewpoint.
(4) The wording must be original, the candidate's rather than the author's.
(5) It must be considerably reduced in length, usually to a prescribed number of words.
(6) It must be so expressed that it reads well and intelligibly even to one who is not aware of the original passage.

Once the relevant part of passage has been thoroughly examined and fully understood, which in this case will have been achieved in the course of dealing with Sections 1 and 2, the next stage is to draw up a plan on which the summary is to be based. What you are aiming for is a plan on the same lines as was described in the chapter on Composition. First start with a title, a brief phrase which will indicate what the whole passage is about. Next, compose sub-titles for what you consider to be the major stages of the argument. If the passage is written in several paragraphs, this paragraph framework could well be used, though it is not always necessary to follow the author's paragraph structure, since much of what he says may be incidental or illustrative matter. Under each sub-title, make a few notes which will act as reminders of the steps in the argument which you will want to bring out. These notes should be in your own words, not the words of the passage, and they should be as brief as possible. It is at this stage that you make your selection of material, discarding anything unnecessary – anything which has already been said, figurative language, illustrations and examples of the point being made, etc. – and leaving only the skeleton of the argument. You must also ensure that only the author's points are included, nothing that belongs to your own attitude rather than his. When all this has been completed, you will have a skeleton plan on which to base your summary.

This planning process can be illustrated from the 1979 passage. (It must be assumed here that the passage is familiar to readers, or that a copy of the past papers is available.)

A reading of this passage reveals that it is about the unique character of every people. Paragraph 1 makes this point at once and gives some examples. Paragraph 2 explains first of all what does *not* cause this uniqueness and then goes on to state what *does*, and how each member of a people passes on that people's characteristics. That part of paragraph 3 which is to be included in the summary makes the point that individual people will always be different from each other but that, if all peoples were brought up in identical environments, then the broad differences would gradually disappear.

Thus there is a clear progression of the argument through the passage, and it is this that must be set down as the plan. This may be done as follows:

The Uniqueness of Peoples
(1) *Uniqueness*
Each has its own combination of characteristics.
(2) *Cause*
Not genetic – environmental – passed on by all members.
(3) *Possibility of change*
Individuality will remain – broad differences could go – identical backgrounds required.

If this is a fair representation of the author's argument, then it should be relatively easy to compose an entirely new passage based on this framework which will in the end say what the author said in a different and shortened form.

Having completed a plan, you can then begin the task of composing the summary. There should now be no need to consult the passage: the notes should be sufficient. In this way you will ensure that the summary is written in your own and not the author's words. From now on you should regard your task as one of ordinary composition, with all that that process involves. You may, however, decide that since the whole passage is going to be rather short there is no need to write in paragraphs. This will depend on the nature of the argument that is to be presented. What you write must be as brief as possible, with no unnecessary flourishes of style. It must, however, be in itself a good piece of prose, written in well-structured sentences, with a proper regard for variety of structures and of sentence length, and good lexical choice. When it is completed, it should read well.

Next we come to the question of length. Some indication of an appropriate length will have been given, probably about a quarter of the length of the original passage, and this figure must be adhered to. In the 1979 paper, the length prescribed was about 70 words. You must, therefore, count the number of words you have used to see how near you have come to the required figure. It is very unlikely that what you have written will fall much below that figure. If it does, you can take it that you have probably omitted something of importance, and should now look for it. Much more probably, you will find that you have written too much. If the difference is slight – up to 5 words, say – you can ignore it. If it is more, you must find some way of reducing the length without destroying the continuity. There may be some long-winded expressions that could be reduced to a single word or a brief phrase; there may be some unnecessary adjectives or adverbs which could be sacrificed without loss; there may be even whole phrases or clauses which could be dropped entirely, such as introductory items like "The writer states that . . .", which should never appear in a summary. If all this fails to reduce the summary to an acceptable length, then there is only one course: you must start again! If this is not possible because of shortage of time, then your summary will be penalised by being marked out of, perhaps, 8 instead of 10. This is a penalty to be avoided, so you must ensure that you have ample time to complete the task.

When eventually you are satisfied that you have written a summary which conforms to all the requirements already listed, then you should, if time permits, make out a fair copy of it since presumably the original will by now contain many alterations which may make it difficult to read. Before doing so, it might be as well to have a last-minute check on the original passage to ensure that nothing has been omitted. When the final version is completed everything else, plan and rough draft, should be clearly crossed out to avoid wasting the examiner's time.

The final step is to add in brackets the number of words you have used in the completed summary. This figure must be as accurate as possible, and it must be honest. If you have written too many words and can find no way around it, then you must be prepared to accept the penalty. Unfortunately, many candidates attempt to cheat on this point by stating a figure that is not true. Excessive length is very obvious to an examiner, and he will deal harshly with any attempt at deception. It is very much in your own interest that you should not risk incurring his displeasure in this way.

Section 4

The areas tested in Section 4 have already been listed as follows:

> the appropriateness of language
> grammatical structure and usage
> the conventions of written English.

As has already been said, not all are necessarily covered in any given year. In fact the nature of the questions set is determined by the nature of the passage. If the passage makes marked use of figures of speech, they will probably figure in the questioning; if the author's word choice is particularly effective or unusual, that will be looked at; if interesting grammatical points occur, you may be asked to comment on them; if punctuation at any point plays an important part in the author's argument that too may figure in the questioning. But it is quite feasible for no questions to occur at all in any of these areas. With such a wide range of possibilities it would be impossible to cover all. The best that can be offered is some general guidelines, illustrated by a few particular examples.

Section 4 goes beyond understanding of simple meaning towards an appreciation of how the author has achieved his effects. Very often this involves his use of visual imagery in order to give to an abstract idea a concrete shape in the reader's mind so that he will be more aware of what the abstract idea means. Various devices can be used to produce the picture desired, and they all have their own special names, such as metaphor, simile and personification. These names may or may not be familiar, but they are not particularly important. What matters chiefly is the term 'image' itself.

When imagery is used, the following questions might be asked about it:

What is the image or picture presented?
Why has it been used?
How well does it enable us to understand the idea?
How suitable is it in the context?

Whenever a question on imagery occurs in the examination, you can be sure that it is concerned with such matters.

In the 1977 passage, for example, the following question was asked:

The author uses an image in the last sentence of paragraph 3.

(i) Explain what the image is, pointing out all the words which contribute to it. (2)
(ii) Comment on its appropriateness in this context. (1)
(iii) How does the author return to this image at a later stage in his argument? (1)

Here four separate tasks are set: to say what picture is suggested by the words, to pick out the words involved, to comment on how well it fits the context, and to find another expression which is connected with it. Taken one at a time, all four are perfectly simple. The image itself is very easily recognised: school is being seen as a prison. The sentence contains two expressions which have obvious connections: "sentence was pronounced" and "the eleven-year stretch". Appropriateness is always a matter of opinion, and anyone is entitled to regard the image as appropriate or inappropriate provided he can support his assertion with argument based on the context. In this case, since the passage is an attack on compulsory attendance at school, it would seem perfectly appropriate for the author to compare the pupil forced to attend school whether he wishes to or not to a person sentenced to 11 years in prison. The final point is very simple: the word "prisons" actually occurs in the last sentence of the passage.

A similar question can be seen in 1978:

> "the wistful revival and gracious laying to rest of some romantic ghost from her own past"

(i) Explain the image used by the author in these words.   (1)
(ii) How effectively do the words chosen help to bring out the nature of the drama he is describing?   (2)

Sometimes questions in Section 4 are concerned with the author's lexical choice – why has he chosen the words he has chosen, and what effect they have apart from their literal meaning.

There are two terms that might be introduced here with some advantage. The first of these is "connotation", a term that may be familiar to many, and one which is very useful. When we talk about the meaning of a word, we are talking of what is denoted by it – what object we think of when we say "table", or what colour we visualise when we say "purple". All words have a denotation of this kind. In addition to its denotation, however, a word may carry other connotations, associated ideas which are brought into our minds when the word is used. Thus the same man may be a staunch Conservative or a dyed-in-the-wool Tory, depending on the political views of the one who is describing him. Both expressions *denote* the same person, but *connote* something entirely different, one an object of approval and the other an object of disapproval. To his friends he may be a fluent speaker: to his enemies he is glib.

Several questions on connotation have been set in past years, though rather fewer recently. One example occurs in 1976:

> What does the word "forging" (line 30) convey about the process of the creation of a new literature?   (1)

With an awareness of what is meant by connotation, such a question should present little difficulty.

The other term which may be found useful is "collocation". This is concerned with the sort of words which one might normally expect to be found in close association with each other. Thus we are not surprised if we find the word 'green' in close proximity to 'grass', 'eye', or 'envy', but we would not normally associated it with 'hair', 'mince', or 'machinery'. 'Love' may frequently be collocated with 'heart', 'tennis' or 'hate', but would not be expected in conjunction with 'typewriter' or 'grammar' or 'examination'. Very often, however, especially in poetry, a writer makes use of unorthodox groupings of words (sometimes known as 'deviant collocation') in order to draw attention to something paradoxical in what he is saying or to give special emphasis to it. Questions on deviant collocation have occurred in the past, but not in recent years. It is always possible, of course, that one will reappear.

Almost everything which is likely to occur in the areas of grammar and punctuation can be dealt with on the basis of what was said on these matters in Chapter One. If we examine a few recent questions we can see that this is so.

1979: The author appears to be asking a question in the sentence beginning "Why had they not resisted . . .?"
How do you know that this question is not the author's?

This is a matter of the verb tense used.

1978: "working class" (line 3); "working-class" (line 15)
Examine each of these expressions in its context and explain clearly the differences between them in terms of grammar and function.

This is a matter of grammar and to a lesser extent punctuation. In the first case, the grammar of the expression is modifier and headword, and its function is as a nominal group. In the second, the compound word formed by the use of the hyphen is an adjective, and it functions as modifier of the headword "origin".

1977: Explain fully why, in your opinion, the author has placed inverted commas round "free" (line 11).

This is concerned with the function of inverted commas to indicate something which is allegedly the case.

1977: Examine carefully the functions of the colons used on lines 17, 20 and 27.

(i)   What phrase used earlier by the author does the colon on line 17 reinforce?
(ii) What is the function of the colon used on line 20?
(iii) The colon on line 27 arouses expectations as to the way in which the sentence will be completed. To what extent are these expectations realised?

This deals with the differing functions of the colon, and in the last case the incomplete nature of what follows the colon.

Obviously, then, those who want to do well in questions of this type should work on Chapter One. No more need be said, apart from the usual warning about the need for care in reading the questions, a need which has already been amply illustrated.

Question B

It was previously said that Question A and Question B are rather different in character, in that Question A is concerned chiefly with meaning and Question B with different varieties of language and the technique used by the writer. This, however, requires modification. As we have seen, Section 4 of Question A has already led us some way into this area, since it is largely concerned with the writer's technique. Much of the knowledge and skill required for the successful tackling of Question B, therefore, has already been discussed under Section 4 and need not be repeated. It should also be realised that in Question B we are coming in to the area known as Practical Criticism. We are familiar with this term in relation to poetry, but it applies equally to prose. It is the technique of close examination of a text in order to see how the writer's intentions have been carried out and his full meaning conveyed by the use of devices beyond the literal meaning of words. Since Practical Criticism occupies an important place in the Literature paper, it will be dealt with fully in the next chapter. Thus all three parts of the paper – Section 4 of Question A, Question B, and Practical Criticism in Paper III – should be seen as closely related, and the corresponding sections of this book should be read in conjunction with each other.

The syllabus describes Question B as one which

". . . will test candidates' awareness of the features of different varieties of English, and their ability to observe the ways in which a difference of purpose in the use of language leads to differences in typography, choice of vocabulary, structuring of material, choice of grammatical forms and other related matters"

The first point to note here is "the features of different varieties of English". Normally Question A is based on a passage of straightforward expository prose; in Question B, however, you must expect a passage written in a register quite different from this. Thus an enormous set of possibilities is opened up – narrative writing, a humorous article, a sermon, an ironical piece, advertising, interior monologue, scientific writing, sports journalism, or any one of the countless varieties of English we encounter regularly. Awareness of different registers, therefore, and of the markers which characterise them is the prime requirement in this section.

The next point to notice is "the ways in which a difference in purpose in the use of language leads to differences in . . .". It is here that we are told that the questions will be based on the writer's technique. Technique is a combination of many factors, the chief of which have already been dealt with: grammar, especially all departures from expected grammatical patterns; punctuation and typographical devices; and lexical choice, especially connotation, collocation and imagery. All that has been written on these subjects should, therefore, be mastered. One other factor is the effect produced by the sound of words. This applies more to poetry than to prose, and will be dealt with in the next chapter, but at this point two devices ought to be mentioned – onomatopoeia and alliteration.

Onomatopoeia is the use of a word or words whose sound is closely related to the meaning. A bell which tinkles, for example, is very different from one which clangs, and birds which twitter are of a different kind from those which scream or those which hoot. Sometimes we can detect that an author has deliberately chosen an expression which is intended to produce this effect. We have a case in question (d) of the 1978 paper, in which candidates were asked to comment on unusual linguistic features in several expressions, one of which was "which rasped you so agreeably all down the spine". Here several points might be made, and one of them could draw attention to the onomatopoeia in "rasped".

Alliteration is an equally well known device. It consists of the repetition of a sound, usually the initial sound of a series of words, designed to draw attention to the words in order to give them some special prominence. In the 1977 passage, candidates were asked to comment on any feature of a book title "Strictly Speaking". One suitable comment would be its alliterative effect.

An examination now of some of the other questions set recently will reveal the sort of thing that is being asked for.

1978: Examine the title of Chapter 1, "OF HIS MALICE AFORETHOUGHT".
  (i)   Of what kind of language is this an example?
  (ii) Point out any language feature which distinguishes it as belonging to this kind of language.

This is a matter of register – the use of archaic or legal terminology – and grammar – the use of a prepositional phrase instead of the adverb "maliciously" and the placing of the adjective after the noun.

> 1978: Why is there a change of verb tense ("stretched"/"had followed") after the opening sentence?

This is a grammatical point. The change of verb tense indicates a switch into the more distant past in order for the author to convey a "flashback".

> 1977: What language feature occurs frequently in paragraph 2 but rarely elsewhere in the passage? Give two examples in support of your answer.

Here the feature which occurs frequently is colloquialism, which is in marked contrast to the rest of the passage.

> 1977: "The Vietnam War was another great spur to woolly thinking to conceal the brutal facts."
> Comment on any incongruity you find in the use in close combination of the three words underlined, and explain how far their use can be justified.

A kind of imagery is involved here in that "spur", "woolly" and "brutal" are all metaphors. The incongruity is that they have been placed together in this way despite the fact that they are so dissimilar – something often called a mixed metaphor. They might be justified, however, on the grounds that the words are so frequently used in this way that they have really ceased to be metaphors – what is sometimes known as decayed metaphor.

> 1977: "to evaluate and make a judgement in terms of a response".
> Replace this with a brief, simple and clear phrase of equivalent meaning.

This is an example of long-winded jargon, which the author is attacking. Far simpler would be something like "to consider an answer".

One special kind of question should be mentioned finally. In 1978 the following appeared:

> The passages set in Questions A and B are very different in purpose, yet there are some similarities in style and tone.

Candidates were then asked to identify the different purposes and go on to discuss which passage was the more attractive in terms of style. It is unusual for a question to be asked concerning both passages, but it is a perfectly legitimate question and is likely to recur. The only warning needed is that you must do more than merely state a preference. You must give reasons for your preference, and these reasons must be based on the author's style of writing. Not only must they be based on style, but all comments must be backed up by examples quoted from the passages. Generalised comments are worthless and will earn no marks.

This, then, is the type of thing that can be expected in Question B. It should be prepared for by a close study of all the sections of this book already mentioned. But of course the true preparation is far more than a mere course of study: it is all the accumulated experience of many years of encountering writings of all kinds, not just "literature".

LITERATURE

The Examination Paper

Paper III is rather different in format from Paper I and Paper II. It is divided into four sections, as follows:

Section 1   – Drama
Section 2   – Prose
Section 3   – Poetry
Section 4   – Practical Criticism

Candidates must attempt three questions, and each question is to be selected from a different section of the paper. Thus it is not possible to choose two questions from, say, the prose section, nor is it possible to make use of all four sections. Within Sections 1, 2 and 3 there is a choice of questions – usually five in each – from which one is to be picked. If Section 4 is chosen, however, all of the questions in it must be answered. All of the questions on the paper carry 20 marks, and so the total mark for the paper is 60. The time allowed is 1 hour 50 minutes, so this means that each answer must be completed in about 35 minutes.

In Sections 1, 2 and 3, questions will be designed to test the candidate's knowledge of the texts he chooses to write about, his ability to marshal his thoughts coherently, and his ability to demonstrate his personal impressions and of reactions to the texts he has chosen. Section 4 is different in that it presents a short text (normally a poem) which will be unknown to the candidate and on this text poses a series of questions designed to test his understanding of its meaning, his awareness of the manner in which it is written, and his competent expression of his own responses to it. Since Section 4 is thus different in character from the other three sections, it will be dealt with separately at the end of this chapter.

Since there are four sections in the paper and only three need be attempted, it would be possible for a student to decide in advance that he will not prepare himself for any one section – that he will read no plays, for example, or that he will take no steps to practise the technique of Practical Criticism. This would be a very unwise decision to make. There is a very practical consideration to be kept in mind here: there is no knowledge in advance which sections will carry questions which can most readily be answered, and therefore no barriers should be erected in advance which will make the task in the examination more difficult. Even more important is the fact that a wide course in literature is the whole basis of training not just for Paper III but for Paper I and Paper II as well. It is our reading which shapes our thinking and it is our reading which teaches us, by example, how to write well. The student who is seriously preparing himself to sit Higher English should base his preparations on as wide a range of reading as he can possibly manage.

A Course of Reading

In Higher English there is no list of prescribed texts on which the examination is based. Questions are so phrased that the candidate must choose from his own reading texts which are suitable as a basis for his answers. No titles of works are ever named on the paper. Since there are no prescribed texts, every candidate must make up his own reading list, ensuring that it is as extensive as possible and covers all kinds of reading.

In choosing suitable works for study, there are several considerations, but these can be reduced to two: the works should be of good literary quality and they should appeal to the reader. This is not the place to attempt a definition of good literary quality. All the texts recommended here will have that quality to some degree. The question of appeal to the reader is very important. If a book is generally recognised as a masterpiece yet fails to give to an individual reader any degree of pleasure or any feeling that it has in some way enriched his life, then it is not a masterpiece for him. It may well be that the fault lies in him for failing to appreciate its merits, but the fact remains that if he is to develop as a reader he must read books which have some message for him. For this reason many people feel that the most suitable books for Higher English candidates are books of the present day or the recent past, or books which, although belonging to an earlier period, still have something of importance to say to people of our times. Shakespeare, of course, has always occupied a special place in the affections of students of English, and for this reason he still figures prominently in most reading lists.

Any selection of attractive books must be a personal selection, and however extensive the list there will always be glaring omissions. The list which follows is such a list. It is not intended to be exhaustive, nor is it intended to be compulsory reading. It is intended merely as a guide to choice. Every text is of at least some literary merit, and all have been proved to have considerable attraction to very many Higher English candidates. All are readily available, either in bookshops or libraries, and almost all can be bought in paperback form.

Drama

Publishers of paperback editions are shown in brackets, except for Shakespeare.

Robert Bolt	— *A Man for All Seasons* (Heinemann)
Arthur Miller	— *A View from the Bridge* (Penguin)
	All my Sons (Penguin)
	Death of a Salesman (Penguin)
	The Crucible (Penguin)
Sean O'Casey	— *Juno and the Paycock* (Macmillan)
	The Plough and the Stars (Macmillan)
John Osborne	— *Look Back in Anger* (Faber)
Harold Pinter	— *The Caretaker* (Methuen)
Shakespeare	— *Hamlet*
	Macbeth
	Othello
	Twelfth Night
Bernard Shaw	— *Pygmalion* (Penguin)
	Saint Joan (Penguin)
Arnold Wesker	— *Roots* (Penguin)

Prose

All are published as Penguins, unless otherwise stated.

Novels

George Douglas	— *The House with the Green Shutters*
Lewis Grassic Gibbon	— *Sunset Song* (Hutchinson)
William Golding	— *Lord of the Flies* (Faber)
Graham Greene	— *Brighton Rock*
	The Power and the Glory
	The Heart of the Matter
Thomas Hardy	— *Far from the Madding Crowd* (Macmillan)
L.P. Hartley	— *The Go-Between*
Ernest Hemingway	— *A Farewell to Arms*
	For Whom the Bell Tolls

Aldous Huxley	– *Brave New World*
D.H. Lawrence	– *Sons and Lovers*
Harper Lee	– *To Kill a Mockingbird*
George Orwell	– *Animal Farm*
	Nineteen Eighty-Four
Alan Paton	– *Cry, the Beloved Country*
J.D. Salinger	– *The Catcher in the Rye*
Alexander Solzhenitsyn	– *One Day in the Life of Ivan Denisovich*
John Steinbeck	– *The Grapes of Wrath*
	Of Mice and Men
Keith Waterhouse	– *Billy Liar*

Prose Non-Fiction

Gerald Durrell	– *My Family and Other Animals*
Robert Graves	– *Goodbye to All That*
Thor Heyerdahl	– *The Kon-Tiki Expedition*
Laurie Lee	– *Cider with Rosie*
George Orwell	– *Down and Out in Paris and London*
	The Road to Wigan Pier

Poetry

K. Allott (ed.)	– *The Penguin Book of Contemporary Verse*
A. Alvarez (ed.)	– *The New Poetry* (Penguin)
R.E.S. Finn (ed.)	– *Poems of the Sixties* (Murray)
R.G. Heath (ed.)	– *Breakthrough* (Hamish Hamilton)
A. MacGillivray &	
J. Rankin (ed.)	– *The Ring of Words* (Oliver and Boyd)
F.T. Palgrave (ed.)	– *The Golden Treasury* (Oxford)
	(The edition 'with a fifth book', ed. J. Press)
G. Summerfield (ed.)	– *Voices (Third Book)* (Penguin)
M. Wollman (ed.)	– *Ten 20th Century Poets* (Harrap)
	Seven Themes in Modern Verse (Harrap)

Note: The individual poets most widely studied by examination candidates are: Wilfred Owen, Ted Hughes, Philip Larkin, Edwin Morgan, Edwin Muir, Norman MacCaig, Robert Browning, John Keats and R. S. Thomas.

These, then, are a few books which ought to give pleasure and some enlightenment. Any number of others can be added at will. But of course whichever books are read, it is not enough merely to read them and enjoy them. There must be some way of thinking about what you read which will help you to derive the maximum benefit from it. What must be realised is that there is no "correct" view to take about any of these books. What is required is a personal response rather than an imposed opinion. Some people find it difficult, however, even to begin evaluating what a book has meant to them. They enjoy the experience and they have feelings about what they have read, but they are unable to put these feelings into words, and they hardly know how to begin to write about them, especially in an examination.

One useful approach is by use of what might be called worksheets. A kind of form can be devised, to be completed for every text studied. On it would be a series of questions which would direct attention to the most important features of the text. Thus the student would build up a collection of sheets, uniform in size and layout, each representing one text, which would be useful both as a means of reaching a full appreciation of the text and as a means of revision at the examination stage. Naturally, not every text would quite fit the formula devised, but the reverse side of the sheet could be used for any additional comments. The sort of worksheet that could be devised can be demonstrated as follows:

DRAMA WORKSHEET

Title.................................   **Date** (approximate) ....

Author...............................   **Nationality** ....

Setting (time).......................   **Setting** (place)........................

Describe any special features of stage technique (use of narrator, flashback, lighting effects, set design, etc.)

Does this method have any particular advantage in this case?

Does the play belong to any special category of drama?

Name the chief character:

What kind of person is he? (*Age, appearance, occupation, character, etc*)

Name a few other important characters, with brief comments.

Is the chief character involved in any kind of conflict? Describe it.

What is the outcome of this conflict? Is it a happy or unhappy outcome?

Mention a few incidents that stand out in your memory. Why?

What, apart from the story, might be said to be the main theme of the play?

Are there any subsidiary themes?

How true to life is the play?

Does the writing have any noticeable features of style?

What was your genuine reaction to this play in terms of both enjoyment and any lesson you may have learned from it?

Do you know any other works dealing with similar themes?

Do you know any other works by the same author?

Additional notes:

NOVEL WORKSHEET

Title ....   **Date** (approximate) ....
Author ....   **Nationality** ....
Setting (time) ....   **Setting** (place) ....

Method of narration
   (a)   Told by chief character in the first person.
   (b)   Told by minor character in the first person.
   (c)   Told by an all-knowing author in the third person.
   (d)   Any other method.

Does the method adopted have any particular advantage in this case?

Does the novel belong to any particular type? (*Fantasy, satire, social realism, science fiction, etc.*)

(The remainder of the novel worksheet could follow exactly the same lines as the drama worksheet).

POETRY WORKSHEET

Title .... **Date** (approximate) ....
Author .... **Nationality** ....

Does the poet write as himself, or does he adopt a persona?

Subject matter (brief outline):

Is there any special significance in the title?

Form (Length, any sub-division into paragraphs or stanzas, rhyme, metre, etc.):

Does it belong to any particular verse form (ballad, sonnet, elegy, etc.)

Does it belong to any particular 'school' of poetry?

Are there any marked features of language? (Register, connotation, imagery, etc.)

Note any words or phrases which seemed especially effective. Why?

What, if anything, makes this poem distinct from all others?

What is its essential message?

What was your genuine reaction to the poem in terms both of enjoyment and any lesson you may have learned from it?

Do you know any other works with a similar theme?

Do you know any other works by the same author?

Additional notes:

With suitable books to read and such a 'do-it-yourself' kit as this worksheet approach, it should not be difficult to build up a knowledge of many texts and a confidence in discussing them. Later, when we come to look at the type of question asked in the examination, you will see that these worksheets cover the ground adequately.

In recent years, many authorities have put forward the view that, while texts can be read as individual works in isolation from all other texts, a great deal of enrichment can be gained by grouping texts together round a common theme – the thematic approach, as it is called. This is an approach which has much to commend it. Every work read adds to what has gone before and leads on to the next, and thus an additional interest is engendered. Works of drama can be related to poems, poetry to novels, and so on. There are great practical advantages too. Many questions in the examination are particularly concerned with theme, and some even ask about a theme which runs through several works, cutting across the Drama/Prose/Poetry boundaries of the first three sections of the paper. There can also be a great carry-over into several other parts of the papers – themes explored can help to form ideas for suitable material for composition, and the study of different approaches to the same theme can help to sharpen awareness of differences of literary technique, thus giving more insight into the 'technical' sections of Paper II and the Practical Criticism section of Paper III. The texts recommended here readily lend themselves to the thematic approach. Orwell's political writings could well lead on to the plays of Wesker, for example, or his *Nineteen Eighty-Four* could be read in conjunction with Huxley's *Brave New World* for two distinctly jaundiced views on how mankind seems to be progressing. Other themes which could well be explored are the nature of childhood and adolescence, racial prejudice, the nature of man – is he inherently good or inherently evil? The poetry anthology *Seven Themes in Modern Verse* may be found especially helpful in this connection.

An extensive programme such as the one described is essential, then, for Higher English. If the texts can be in some way thematically linked, so much the better. The worksheet method should be considered and adopted if found useful. Whether or not this method is adopted, however, some kind of programme of writing about the texts read is necessary if you are to be prepared for the examination.

Sections 1, 2 and 3

Choosing the Questions

All the questions in the first three sections of Paper III are so worded that the candidate himself must choose the text or texts which he will use as the basis of his answers. There are never any references to specific works. In fact, there are not even any references to specific authors, with the one exception of Shakespeare, whose name always appears in the first two questions of Section 1. Even in these questions, however, no specific plays are mentioned. Candidates must choose from their knowledge of Shakespeare a play which is suited to the exact demands of the question. Although these first two questions are always based on Shakespeare's plays, there is nothing to prevent any of the other drama questions being answered on a Shakespeare play, provided that the wording of the questions does not exclude him – by referring to a twentieth century playwright, for example.

With as many as fifteen or sixteen questions on the paper and only three to be chosen, it is obviously vital that the selection of the three should be done quickly and wisely. Speed is important simply because there is so little time available, but it is equally important to make a wise choice. You must read each question quickly but carefully in order to be sure that you know exactly what it is asking for. It will not simply be asking about a text: it will be singling out some particular topic and asking you to discuss that topic on the basis of the text or texts you choose. Many candidates go astray here, but in two separate directions. Some write reasonably well about the topic but fail to discuss it in terms of a specific text, while others display considerable knowledge of texts without making any reference to the terms of the question. Both errors have equally disastrous consequences. All answers must be based on texts, and all answers must deal with the precise demands of the question.

Having read and understood the question, you must then decide if you know any texts which will fit the requirements of the question. If you do not, then you can pass on to the next question. If you do, you must consider how well the text you have chosen fits the question and how well you know it. You need not know it in every last detail, but you must have an intelligent understanding of its basic theme, and a reasonably sound recollection of all its features. It should also be a text which has made a strong impression on you, one which you would enjoy writing about. Once you have found a question which fits these requirements you can mark it as a possibility.

The wisest policy now is to examine quickly each of the three sections, and in each case decide finally which one question you will attempt if in the end you decide to choose that section. Thereafter, you can completely forget about the remaining questions. Next you have to consider the Practical Criticism section as a possibility. Factors influencing your choice here will be discussed in the appropriate place. If you reject this option, then you can begin work on the questions you have already selected. If, on the other hand, you decide to attempt Section 4, then you must decide quickly which of the other three now to discard – presumably the one which gave you least confidence in your ability to answer it or the one which seemed least attractive to you.

What is being recommended, then, is that you should know before you start work on any one question exactly which three questions you are going to attempt. It is not wise to choose one question and answer it before making the next choice, and then repeating this at the end of what will have been a very exhausting day. Many who do this make very rash final choices, and their papers peter out disastrously. If you know in advance what you are going to do, you can tackle each task with confidence, secure in the knowledge that you will be able to approach the next task with equal confidence. If you have made your choice as speedily as possible – ideally, in five minutes – then you can allocate your time properly so that all questions are given an equal and sufficient amount of time. The questions can then be taken in any order starting with the one which interests you most.

As a reminder, here are the three questions which you should ask yourself before selecting a question:

> Do I know any text which will fit the question?
> Do I know it well enough?
> Has it had sufficient impact on me?

Planning The Answer

There are several factors that go to make up a good answer on a literature question. These may be listed as follows:

1. The relevance of the answer to the specific topics raised in the question.
2. The way in which knowledge of texts is displayed.
3. The suitability of the text chosen.
4. The quality of genuineness in discussing personal reactions to the texts.
5. The literary qualities of the answer.

The factors are all very important, but at the moment we shall be concerned chiefly with the first three – relevance, textual knowledge, and suitability of text.

In order to ensure that all these requirements are met, some degree of planning is necessary. Time is short, of course, but unless a plan is followed the answer will be completely shapeless and may not fully meet these essential requirements. A paragraph plan must therefore be drawn up as quickly and as efficiently as possible. The obvious method to use is that which was described in Chapter Two – a general title, paragraph sub-titles, and paragraph notes.

The choice of a title here can be of great help in directing the mind to the fundamental point of the question, thus ensuring relevance. A close inspection of any question will reveal this fundamental point. For example, Question 5 (1978) reads as follows:

> Select two features (e.g. setting, character, lighting, plot, music, etc.) from a play you found enjoyable. Demonstrate, using clear reference to the text, that each would make a strong contribution to the meaning and/or the atmosphere of the play if it were seen in production.

This is clearly a question on stage technique. This should be kept firmly in mind. Therefore if we adopt a title such as *Music and Flashback Technique* in *Death of a Salesman* we shall ensure that this is the topic dealt with in our answer. Another example can be seen in Question 8 in the same paper:

> Select a novel in which you found a thought-provoking theme. Discuss what part its plot played in conveying the theme, and to what extent it was conveyed by other means (e.g. setting, characters, imagery, etc.)

This asks for the identification of a theme and an evaluation of the contribution made by the plot to the theme in relation to that made by any other aspect or aspects of the play. This we can ensure by adopting the title "Evil Conveyed by Plot and Character in *Brighton Rock*".

Question 15 in 1978 read as follows:

> Choose a poem you have studied in depth, and illustrate what features of the poet's use of language made the poem distinctive and memorable for you.

Clearly this question is about poetic technique and the ways in which a poet makes use of striking language. A title to cover this might be '*The Technique of Surprise in "Thrushes" by Ted Hughes.*' The title chosen is not necessarily for inclusion in the answer – though it would be of advantage to include it – so it need not be a particularly brief or a particularly clever one, but it must direct attention to the phrase that matters in the question. The practice followed by many candidates of copying out the whole question at the head of their answer is not one to be recommended. It is this key phrase that matters.

Next we come to the logical structure of the answer. This can best be ensured by a sub-division into paragraphs, just as is done in a composition.

The general title has directed attention to the broad subject-matter of the answer: paragraph sub-titles direct attention to the particular steps in the argument. These sub-titles, however, should in no circumstances be introduced into the answer as headings. They are part of the plan only, and the answer must make use of normal topic sentences and linking devices. Again the question should be studied closely in order to ensure that all parts of it are covered in the plan. Most questions, in fact, are so worded that they give a clear indication of a suitable paragraph structure. Consider, for example, the three questions already mentioned. First there was the question on stage technique. The first sentence defines the kind of play that is to be discussed. This could correspond to an opening paragraph which names the text chosen and gives a brief indication of reasons for the choice. The second sentence asks about the ways in which the technique is used, and this will form the basis of the main bulk of the answer – a series of perhaps two paragraphs each dealing with one aspect of technique. This sentence also asks for an impression of the effect of the technique. This should lead to a final paragraph in which the candidate sums up what he has said and gives his personal judgement on it. Thus a set of useful sub-titles might be:

1. Choice of *Death of a Salesman*
2. Flashback technique
3. The use of music
4. Personal impressions.

The second question was about the contribution of plot and character to the theme of a novel. The following plan meets all the terms of the question:

1. Theme of evil in *Brighton Rock*
2. Superficial story
3. Pinkie's choice of evil
4. Contrast with Ida Arnold
5. Contrast with Rose
6. Final damnation – evil complete.

The poetry question was on the use of striking language features, and was directed at technique rather than subject-matter. This could be dealt with as follows:

1. The surprise quality in *Thrushes*
2. Word Choice
3. Sentence Structure
4. Sound effects
5. Contribution to full understanding.

The next requirement that has to be met is a sufficient demonstration of textual knowledge. Already we have guaranteed by the choice of title and sub-titles that our answers will be relevant and based on texts. The notes added to the sub-titles should be so designed that every point that is made in the argument is substantiated by reference to particular parts of the text. Thus for our drama answer we might note under flashback technique some reminders of particular instances – Willy Loman remembering his interview with his boss, Biff on his way to the football game, the constant coming-back to the woman in the hotel. Under 'music' we could mention the flute tune, with its suggestion of the open air, and Ben's theme. For *Brighton Rock* we would again pick out references to use – Pinkie's up-bringing and belief in evil, Ida Arnold's feeling for the murdered man and her sense of right and wrong. Rose's innocence yet willingness to do evil for Pinkie's sake, Pinkie's death without the possibility of repentance, and the final irony of his recorded message of hatred left behind for Rose to hear. For *Thrushes* particular expressions would be listed for discussion.

Thus the paragraph plans for these three questions that finally emerge could be as follows:

Music and Flashback Technique in *Death of a Salesman*
1. Choice of *Death of a Salesman:*
   unusual techniques – flashback, music
2. Flashback technique:
   interview with Howard – Biff's football – woman in hotel.
3. The use of music:
   flute tune – Ben's theme
4. Personal impressions:
   confusing at first but effective.

Evil conveyed by plot and characters in *Brighton Rock*
1. Theme of evil:
   Can be read on different levels
2. Superficial story:
   Thriller-type story – gangs, murder, pursuit, etc.
3. Pinkie's choice of evil:
   Sordid background – escape through crime – belief in hell.
4. Contrast with Ida Arnold:
   Her feeling for Hale – sense of right and wrong.
5. Contrast with Rose:
   Her goodness – yet willingness to commit sin.
6. Final damnation.
   Death (cliff, bottle of vitriol) – no repentence – irony of gramo-phone record left for Rose – positive evil proved.

The Technique of Surprise in *Thrushes* by Ted Hughes
1. The surprise quality in *Thrushes*:
   Word choice, sentence structure, sound.
2. Word choice:
   Metaphors of violence – trigger, stab, steel – terrifying – the shark and the 'blood-smell' – 'orgy and hosannah'.
3. Sentence structure:
   Verbless sentences – 'Nothing but bounce . . .', 'No indolent . . .' – Final complex sentence.
4. Sound effects:
   'poised with dark deadly eye', 'some writhing thing', 'heroisms on horseback', wilderness/water/weep.
5. Contribution to full understanding:
   Deadly nature – opposite of conventional picture. Contrast of thrush with man. "Distinctive and memorable."

These, of course, are only three examples, and only suggested ways of treating them. No doubt many better plans could be devised. The point is that it is only by adopting some plan and carrying it out that the first two basic requirements of an answer will be met – that it answers the question and that it is based on the text. The third requirement, that of suitability, has also been met in the course of this planning. In each case, ample material has been assembled to frame a sound answer. It follows, therefore, that the texts chosen were suitable. As many other questions as possible should now be studied, and in each case some attempt should be made to see how a similar plan could be devised.

Composing the Answer

A good paragraph plan should ensure that the first three requirements of an answer are met. The other two must be borne in mind while the answer is being composed. These are the sincerity of the comments offered and the literary skill demonstrated in the answer.

Sincerity is very important. What is always looked for is a completely frank answer to the question showing the impact the text has actually made on you. Literature answers should always show that the experience of reading has been one which has given both pleasure and enlightenment. The questions are in no way suited to any kind of cramming course which has as its aim the preparation of accepted critical opinions, character sketches, plot summaries, and so on. The views you express may not be those of the examiner, and they may well offend against accepted critical opinion, but these things will not be held against you if what you say reveals that the text you are writing about has really meant something to you. There is nothing so depressing as an answer which has clearly been rehearsed, which obviously represents not what the candidate thinks but what he has been told to think, and which is even written in words which are not his own – words borrowed from someone else's 'notes' or from the introduction to a book. This type of answer, unfortunately, is all too common, and it is always treated with severity. Many such answers, incidentally, are not merely rehearsed in advance – they are patently memorised. As a result of using such answers, most candidates are guilty of serious irrelevance, which counts heavily against them in the assessment.

The only way to guard against this is to be sure that you enter the examination with no preconceived notions on what you are going to write about and what you are going to say. You must approach the questions in the way described in the section 'Choosing the Questions'. You must then prepare to answer them in the way described in the section 'Planning the Answer'. If you do that, and then go on to compose an answer with some literary skill, you should do well.

The final factor that decides how good an answer is is the way in which it has been expressed. An answer which meets all the other requirements but is not in itself a good piece of English writing may deserve a pass, but it will not score such a high mark as one which adds to the other qualities some signs of literary skill. The planning should have helped some way towards this in that it should have guaranteed sound material presented in a logical way – the first requirements of good writing. But to that must be added all the other ingredients that were described in Chapter Two – well structured paragraphs properly linked together, competent sentence structure which contains adequate variety, and skilful lexical choice. All of these should be kept in mind in composing your answer. Each answer is, after all, a composition in itself and should be treated as such. Although all the normal rules of good composition apply here, what you can write in half an hour will, of course, be much less than what you would produce in a full-scale composition. For most people the normal length of answer is about 200–300 words, though length itself is not of prime importance. Within the limits of that length, what you produce must have the characteristics of a good composition twice its length.

There is no need to repeat all that was said on composition in Chapter Two. It must be assumed that it was all properly understood and digested. Only a few points that arise particularly in writing about literature need be mentioned.

The first of these is the way that your answer should begin. Already the use of a title has been recommended, preferably one which can be included as part of the answer. If you do use it in your answer, however, you must realise that it is separate from the answer. The opening sentence of the answer must make its own sense without requiring of the reader any knowledge of the title or of the wording of the question. It would not do to open with:

'A play which fits this description is . . .'
'One such novel is . . .'
'This is a poem which . . .'

Instead, the opening sentence should make clear what the topic is and give some indication of how it is going to be treated. Thus:

'One of the most attractive features of *Death of a Salesman* by Arthur Miller is the fact that it is highly original in some of the techniques it employs.'
'Although at one level *Brighton Rock*, by Graham Greene, can be enjoyed simply as a thriller, at a deeper level it can be seen to be concerned with a very important theme, that of the nature of evil'.
'A poem which is particularly striking in its language features is *Thrushes*, by Ted Hughes'.

In each case, the opening sentence has introduced the topic to be discussed – the topic that features in the question – and has named a text (and an author) which will serve to illustrate the topic. The remainder of this opening paragraph, which can be quite brief, perhaps no more than one sentence, may go on to give some indication of the manner in which the topic is to be treated:

'Probably its outstanding feature is its use of the flashback, but its originality can also be seen in Miller's introduction of particular musical effects to fit his purpose.'
'In the person of its chief character, Pinkie, Greene has attempted to create someone who has in him absolutely no trace of goodness'.
'We can see this if we consider only three aspects of the poem: the choice of words, the sentence structures involved, and the use of sound.'

When the successive paragraphs are being written it must be remembered that they are all steps in the discussion of the central issue, the topic that has been extracted from the question and stated in the opening sentence. A continuity of argument can be ensured if into the topic sentence of every paragraph the key phrase, or preferably some variation of it, can be introduced. In this way, there will be no problem of irrelevance. For example:

> 'The flashback technique is common enough in films, but its use in a stage play is certainly very unusual.'
> 'Although the actual plot is admittedly unimportant when compared with the underlying theme, nevertheless it is in itself very attractive.'
> 'This striking quality is most clearly seen in *Thrushes* when we look at some of the words Hughes has chosen to use.'

This continual coming back to the terms of the question, provided it is not done to excess, will help to give a firm direction to everything that is said, and it should be kept in mind at the very end too, when a final reiteration of the essential phrase that has been under discussion should ensure that the whole essay has been led to a successful conclusion.

There remains one other matter – the introduction of quotations. We have already seen the need for an adequate demonstration of knowledge of the text, and the use of quotation can certainly help here. But there should be three limitations: quotations should be few, they should be brief, and they should be an apt illustration of what is being said. Certainly in poetry questions quotation will be necessary, but in prose and drama there is not the same need. In discussing poetry, the actual words used must be referred to, but in other cases it is usually sufficient to refer to characters and incidents without quoting the words used, unless they are in some way outstanding. Nothing should ever be memorised in advance with a view to quotation: only items which remain in the mind should be used. The idea should be to use quotation not as a matter of policy but only if something springs to mind as being exactly the right thing to say in the circumstances.

Some people have difficulty in introducing their quotations. They make a statement, and after it they baldly set down a quotation without saying why they are doing so or in any way connecting it with their own sentence. If quotations are to be introduced, they must be properly introduced. A short quotation, a single word or a phrase, becomes simply a part of the sentence in which it is written. It is not introduced by a colon or set on a new line. It is simply enclosed in inverted commas, as follows:

> "During Act One of 'Hamlet' we are constantly being reminded that 'something is rotten' in society."
> "The 'terrible beauty' that Yeats refers to is a reflection of his own attitude to the events of 1916."

A longer quotation must be introduced differently. It needs to be introduced by a statement followed by a colon. Then the quotation is set on a new line, and enclosed in inverted commas:

> "Consider, for example, the sentence structure in the following lines from *Thrushes*:
> 'No indolent procrastinations and no yawning stares,
> No sighs or head-scratchings. Nothing but bounce and stab
> And a ravening second.' "

Special Questions

There are two types of question which deserve some special notice, what might be termed 'thematic' and 'technique' questions.

The syllabus informs us that 'candidates who have studied literature thematically will be provided with opportunities to use in answers the kind of understanding resulting from such a method.' Throughout the paper there are questions which are concerned chiefly with the theme which underlies a work, but in addition there are some questions which deal with the treatment of a theme in several works, cutting across the division of the paper into drama, prose and poetry. At least one such question will normally be found, and it can be expected as the last question in any section. The treatment of such questions is for the most part exactly as has already been described, but there are a few special points to notice.

First of all you must note how many texts you are to refer to and what type of texts they are to be. Then you must determine which is to be the major text discussed. This will normally be clear from the wording of the question, but if there is any doubt you should realise that the decisive factor is the section in which the question has been placed. If it is in the Prose section, then a prose text should be chosen for major attention, with drama or poetry texts used to support the argument and provide further illustration. Having decided that one text is the major text, you must ensure that your answer has the proper proportions. Discussion of that text should form the major part of your answer, but at the same time there must be at least adequate treatment of a minor text, not just a passing reference. When choosing texts for discussion, it would not be legitimate to choose one which is the basis of one of your other answers on the paper. Admittedly this is not specifically prohibited, but it is a clear evasion of one of the requirements of the paper – some evidence of wide reading – and will be taken as an indication of, to say the least, a lack of interest in the subject and treated accordingly. Examples of such thematic questions can be seen in 1979, question 10, and in 1977, question 5.

Questions on the writer's technique will also be encountered in the paper, especially in the Poetry section. These are questions not about the content of a text but about the ways in which the writer has constructed his work. The question already discussed with *Death of a Salesman* as a text is an example of such a question in drama, and features such as those mentioned in the suggested plan would be legitimate considerations here. Other factors that could be discussed might be the way in which the author moves his characters on and off the stage, his use of various dramatic climaxes and curtains, his variation of the number of characters present, the quality of his dialogue, his use of stage directions, etc. An example of a technique question in prose can be seen in 1979, question 7, which is concerned, among other things, with "a crucial incident, character, setting, quality of language etc." Other matters of those prose technique might be the use of setting, dialogue, description, dramatic conflict, figurative language, symbolism, chapter or other divisions, etc. A typical technique question in poetry is the one which has already been quoted, the question dealing with striking language features. This question actually listed some of the topics which are matters of technique:

"You may wish to refer to such features as choice of words, unusual combination of words, imagery, structure, rhythm, verse form, etc."

Question 13 in the 1979 paper offers some more help:

"You may wish to refer to word choice, structure, imagery, etc."

The examiners do not expect all candidates to tackle these technical questions. This is made clear in the syllabus:

"Little formal knowledge of literary history as such or the technicalities of prose or poetry will be expected in the candidates' answers. However credit will be given for thorough knowledge of the selected texts, awareness of the techniques used, sincerity of personal response, competence in written English, and evidence of wide and independent reading."

Unfortunately, all too many candidates do attempt these questions, often with an inadequate idea of the kind of knowledge that is required to answer them. They are all good and rewarding questions to attempt, but only for those with that knowledge. They should be ignored by all others.

Irrelevance

The importance of being relevant has already been stressed repeatedly, and various precautions have been suggested to ensure that this is achieved. Unfortunately, however, there is always a very large number of candidates who are found to be at fault in this respect, and the consequence is, almost inevitably, failure. Probably the chief reasons for falling into this trap are carelessness in reading the question and the determination, come what may, to use in the examination material which has been prepared beforehand. Both of these dangers have already been mentioned, and it is impossible to over-stress them.

As in composition, there are different degrees of irrelevance, and they deserve different penalties. Unlike the Composition paper, however, the Literature paper can attract answers which are so grossly irrelevant that they deserve no marks at all. When a candidate is asked to write about a poem and instead writes about a novel (presumably because he knows no poems) then even with the best will in the world no examiner can give him any marks. Incredibly enough, this is what some people do. If a question asks for a comparison of two texts and only one is offered, this may not be entirely valueless since there may at least be some knowledge of the text displayed. The terms of the question have not even remotely been met, however, so such an answer could hardly earn more than a token two or three marks. Again incredibly enough, this happens too. If the question is about, say, prose non-fiction and is answered on a novel, this is not quite as serious a crime. At least the prose form has been chosen, and if the novel comes near to meeting the terms of the question it may earn rather more marks – but hardly a pass. These, then, are the worst cases – cases where the basic fault lies in the wrong selection of texts. They serve to illustrate the importance of making a good choice.

The vast bulk of cases of irrelevance, however, is found among those who choose a perfectly acceptable text but then fail to deal with the question adequately. The worst of these are those who ignore the question almost entirely – who tell the story of the play, or present a character sketch of the hero of the novel, or who give an appreciation of their favourite poem, regardless of what exactly they were asked to do. These are usually the people with prepared answers, and they must fail, though they will be given some credit for the knowledge they display and the skill with which they express it. Other candidates – a very large number – do attempt to answer the question but fail to deal with all the points raised. Some phrase in the question may have escaped their notice, or they may have thought it unimportant. Such cases deserve to be treated more sympathetically. While they must be penalised for not completing their task, they may well deserve to pass if their answers show enough of the other essential characteristics of a good answer. Indeed, if their work is particularly good, they may still score a very comfortable pass, but it will not be as high a mark as it would have been if the terms of the questions had been fully met. No one can afford the loss of even two or three marks, so you must be on your guard.

If, however, an answer is produced which is entirely relevant and which deals with all aspects of the question asked, then a pass mark is virtually assured. If the text is adequately referred to in the answer, then the pass is guaranteed. A well-structured, logical answer will raise the mark even higher into a very comfortable position. If there is clear evidence that the candidate has been genuinely moved by what he has read and has been able to convey his reactions sincerely, then his mark should now be of A quality (70% = 14 out of 20). On top of all this, if the quality of his writing is of some literary merit, then there is nothing to prevent him scoring a very high mark indeed – for the very talented and literate candidate, nothing to prevent him achieving full marks.

Section 4 – Practical Criticism

The Nature of the Question

An optional question on Practical Criticism was introduced into the Higher English paper in 1970 in order to allow candidates a chance to demonstrate, in addition to their knowledge of texts they had studied, their ability to evaluate a text that was completely new to them. The text set has up to the time of writing always been a fairly short poem, although the syllabus allows for the possibility of using occasionally a piece of prose or dramatic dialogue either instead of a poem or as an alternative to it. The kind of ability required is the same for all three, however, and throughout this section only poetry will be referred to.

The syllabus shows us that the question is intended to test candidates in three ways:

'Answers to questions will be expected to show an understanding of the meaning of the text, an appreciation of the manner in which it is written, and ability to express, in acceptable forms, the candidates' own responses to the text'.

In many ways, of course, these aims are the same as those of Paper II. The text, however, will be of a more strongly 'literary' quality, and so there will be less emphasis on its simple meaning and more on the way in which the meaning is fully brought out. In other words, the test will consist of a series of questions on literary technique. This is an area which is already familiar to us through Section 4 of Question A in Paper II, Question B in the same paper, and the 'technique' questions in the first three sections of paper III.

Practical Criticism should never be regarded as an easy alternative to the essay type of question. A considerable amount of knowledge, skill and sensitivity is called for, and not all candidates possess these qualities. Unfortunately it is chosen by many who lack the skill to do it well, and as a result they fare very badly. Generally speaking, a candidate of average ability should, by careful attention to the demands of the question, manage to score somewhere around half marks in the questions in Sections 1, 2 and 3, but the same candidate, unless he is properly prepared, may fall far below the pass level in Section 4. On the other hand, a candidate of above-average ability who can manage a very comfortable pass in the other sections can do even better in Section 4, with marks shooting up right to the highest level. The best advice to give, therefore, is that those who know that they have to struggle to scrape up a pass in the paper should avoid Practical Criticism, whereas those who know from experience that they have some talent in this field should be more than willing to choose this question.

Before turning to Section 4, of course, everyone should already have three other questions earmarked for possible treatment. Some, if they accept the advice given above, will look no further and take these as their final choice. Others, who know that they may be able to do this question well, will now have to make a decision. The text should be read through fairly quickly to see if it has any particular attraction, and then the questions should be looked at to see if they offer any interesting possibilities. You cannot expect, of course, that everything will be clear at once. If it were, the text would not have been set in the examination. You may indeed find it rather difficult at first, but if it excites any interest then it will deserve a closer look. If after that closer look you feel that you are developing a fuller understanding, and if you find that the questions seem to be within your capabilities, you would be well advised to choose this question and discard one of the other three.

Throughout your work on this section you must concentrate on the exact wording of the questions in order to answer them fully, and you must remember that everything you write must be firmly based on the words of the text. General impressions are not called for: what is required is a detailed comment which is always supported by reference to the text. This last point is particularly important – support everything you say by reference to the words of the poem.

In order to equip yourself properly to tackle this question successfully, you must be sure that you are aware of what constitutes literary technique. Some of this ground has already been covered, but now it is necessary for the subject to be treated rather more fully. *The remainder of this

106

chapter will be given over to a description of some of the technical devices likely to be encountered. Frequent reference will be made to the poems set in 1978 and 1979, and for convenience they are reprinted here.

LAKE SCENE

Built on conveyor belts,
They move along conveyor belts of tarmac.
Machines that graze on
Mountain, wood, and lake,
Pasture and ploughland, even

Homes and houses of men, and
The cities where they've come from.
Bobbles of painted metal,
Volvo, Ford, Rover, Datsun
– Silica gleam of locust-swarm –

Flip by a leafshaped lake
As good as any colour transparency;
Soft romantic mountains, framed
In a thousand windscreens daily,
And places like this, seen to death;

Or stop – and out come folding
Tables, chairs; plastic thermos;
Cups, plates, polythene cake,
Dog on leash, portable telly.
Awed, lakes and hills retreat.

David Wright

---

* An even fuller account of the subject can be found, if required, in my book, '*Practical Criticism*', also published by Gibson. Ample practice material can be found in '*Exercises in Practical Criticism*'.

BAVELAW IN WINTER

Searching late for a Bronze Age cairn
I saw the reservoir glittering through
A row of blackened pinewood: it formed
A cretin's gaptoothed grin through which
Cold winds drew breath for bleak syllables
On the subject of desolation
Pewter clouds raced over skull-shaped
Hills and mangled what was left of sky

Place and time felt warped out of focus
The city behind me hid under its own
Miasma like a threatened squid
And it seemed the peat-hag riddled moor
Could sprout a herd of mastodon
Almost I saw them troop across Golgotha
And heard instead of burbling curlew
A pterodactyl tear the wind to shreds

And rearing huge in the bloodshot eye
Of the sun tyrannosaurus rex
Grappling with annihilation
Where druids flared up antique festivals
And now asthmatic sheep turn up collars
Against the winds of night,
I turn up mine and head for home
A Bronze Age cairn will keep till spring

Stanley Roger Green

Situation

One of the first things we should notice about any poem is the situation on which it is based. Often there will be no particular situation – merely a poet reflecting on some aspect of life. Many poems, however, are clearly based on a particular experience or event, and an awareness of this can sometimes be an aid to understanding. Examination of the poem should begin, then, with a consideration of who is speaking, to whom is he speaking, and what are the circumstances surrounding him.

Sometimes, of course, there will be virtually nothing that could be called 'speaking', and the word 'I' will not occur. In such a case we could say simply that the poet is addressing his words to his readers. On other occasions the poem will be a clear form of address, indicated by the use of the first person. When this occurs, we must be sure who is represented by 'I'. It may be the poet himself directly addressing us about an experience, but it may also be some 'persona', a character invented by the poet through whom his words will reach us. Again, the persona may be directly addressing us, or he may be addressing some third party – or even speaking to himself. If he is speaking to another person who replies to him, we could describe this as dialogue; if he is speaking to a person who clearly exists but does not participate in the speech we may call this dramatic monologue; if he is speaking to himself he is indulging in soliloquy.

If we discover that the poem consists of some form of address, either by the poet or by a persona, we should then consider the register employed to see how well it fits the situation. Things we might look for are the degree of formality or informality present, or any markers that might indicate the speaker's occupation or character or the nature of the subject. It will be especially interesting if we discover any change that may occur in the register employed, because this may indicate some development in the thought of the poem.

With these ideas in mind, we can look at our two poems. In *Bavelaw in Winter* there is a direct address, since 'I' is used in the second line. There is also a particular incident involved, since the speaker says:

> "Searching late for a Bronze Age cairn
> I saw the reservoir . . ."

Later on the use of 'and now' indicates a present event – he is surveying a hostile landscape and deciding that if the cairn has been there since the Bronze Age it will still be there in a few months' time if he returns in more pleasant weather conditions. There is nothing to suggest here that any persona has been adopted, so presumably we have the poet himself addressing us. This would fit with the register employed. It might be described best as a neutral register, with no marked colloquial or other features – the language of educated, literary communication in writing, which is exactly what the poem is. Significantly in this case, the questions set on the poem reflect this absence of any strongly marked persona or register by virtually ignoring this area, apart from question (b) (iii), which draws attention to the change which occurs in the author's reaction to the landscape around him.

Lake Scene has a much less clearly defined situation. Here there is no "I". The writer is simply addressing his readers to make a comment on a feature of modern life – the conflict between modern "plastic" technology and the natural beauty of the countryside. It is interesting to note a marked change in register when in lines 16–19 we are offered a list of everyday useful articles, typical of our times. This is then followed by the last line:

"Awed, lakes and hills retreat."

This contrast is what lies behind question (d), which asks how effective this last line is in summing up the meaning of the poem.

Grammatical Features

Apart from the literal and figurative meaning of the words the poet has chosen, some contribution to meaning is often made by non-lexical features which can loosely be termed 'grammatical'. An awareness of grammar and punctuation can be particularly helpful whenever there is any departure from the usage which might be expected. This usually indicates something of significance. Much of this ground has already been covered with reference to Question B of Paper II. All that is required here is to look at our two poems with this feature in mind.

One interesting thing occurs right at the beginning of "Lake Scene". In line 2 the poet says "They move . . ." Normally a personal pronoun is used only after the thing it stands for has been named – "There is a steady stream of cars. They move . . ." Here, no such word as "cars" has been used. The reader must supply it for himself, and he cannot do this until he has read some way into the poem. Then he will come back to the title and will grasp its full significance.

Lines 3–7 read:

"Machines that graze on
Mountain, wood, and lake,
Pasture and ploughland, even

Homes and houses of men, and
The cities where they've come from."

There are several interesting points of grammar here. For example, there is the use of the singular form in "Mountain, wood, and lake", where we would normally expect the plural. The effect is as if cars are destroying not just some of the countryside but all of it. Then there are some distinct groupings presented in a parallel way: first the natural scenery, then the agricultural land, and finally the urban environment – an all-embracing destructiveness. This is further intensified by the placing of the word "even" at the very end of the first paragraph, leaving a pause which gives added emphasis to the next two lines.

110

Later the cars are listed:

"Volvo, Ford, Rover, Datsun"

Again they are in the singular, but there is no "and" to link them together. It is as if the list might be endless. Then there is an insertion, marked off by dashes, between the list of cars which is the subject of the sentence and the verb "Flip". This draws attention to the insertion, with its unusual word combinations and its encapsulation of the destructive nature of the car.

In the last stanza we have three lines in which we read a list of the material possessions which to the poet seem to have corrupted modern society. The list is presented without connectives and without the article "a" in cases where it might be expected. Again, it is as if the list could go on for ever.

In the last line, the word order is unusual, with "Awed" coming first rather than "lakes and hills", and the use of the comma puts additional emphasis on the opening word, thus making us even more aware of the way in which modern "progress" has destroyed nature.

In "Bavelaw in Winter" there are fewer points of grammatical interest. Here the interest is more in the poet's choice of words. The punctuation, however, is interesting. For his own reasons – perhaps because of the nightmarish quality of the experience he is describing – the poet has chosen to write his lines almost without punctuation, leaving the reader to determine for himself where all the stops come. There are two marks of punctuation however. There is a colon in the middle of line 2. Previous to this, the poet has explained the situation: during a search on Bavelaw for a Bronze Age cairn he came across a striking view. After the colon we have the unpunctuated nightmarish thoughts that this view inspired in him. But at the end of line 22 there is a comma, indicating that the reflections are over. There is a kind of deflation as we return to normality, the poet simply turning up his collar against the cold and deciding to go home and wait till weather conditions are better. Thus the two marks of punctuation have an important part to play in the structure and meaning of the poem.

These are only a few of the features of grammar that may attract our attention in poetry. Whenever anything unusual occurs, we should examine it closely and we will usually find something significant underlying the feature we have observed.

Lexical Features
The main weight of the meaning of a poem, of course, is carried by the words themselves, what they mean and what additional meanings they suggest to us. A great deal has already been said about good lexical choice,

and this is the outstanding feature of most poetry. Words used must be effective and appropriate, and in poetry they must be particularly so since poetry is a very condensed form of expression, often revealing layers of meaning unnoticed at a superficial reading.

The chief means by which additional layers of meaning are added are connotation, unusual collocation, and the use of imagery. These were explained and illustrated in the last chapter. One other device needs to be added here – the use of deliberate ambiguity, or multiple meaning. In normal communication ambiguity is thought of as a fault. If our utterances are to be effective, people must not be left in doubt as to what we mean. In poetry, however, this is not necessarily the case. Sometimes there are different levels of meaning that the poet wants to convey. The case of "warped" in "Bavelaw in Winter" is one example. It means literally twisted or distorted, but at the same time it carries the idea of the "time warp" common in science fiction, and so it prepares us for the poet's imaginative leap into the ancient past. The use of ambiguity is one of the most powerful techniques used by poets to produce work which is densely packed with meaning.

If we were to subject our two poems to a minute analysis of lexical features, we could go on almost indefinitely. Every word that carries meaning has been chosen deliberately in preference to the virtually infinite number of words that could have been chosen and every one could warrant scrutiny, but we cannot be as painstaking as that. We must be content with only the outstanding features, chiefly those which are referred to in the questions set.

"Lake Scene" opens with an immediate surprise. The connotations of the title are of natural beauty and peacefulness, yet at once we find ourselves reading about conveyor belts. Then the literal conveyor belts of line 1 become in line 2 the figurative "conveyor belts of tarmac", suggesting that the whole countryside has become one vast production line. The imagery then changes as the cars become "machines that graze". The word "graze" normally has pleasant pastoral connotations, but in this case we find that what is being eaten up is the whole landscape, both rural and urban. Thus within the first few lines we have strikingly been made aware of the poet's attitude to modern man as he despoils the land with his material possessions. The grazing imagery is repeated on line 10 with "locust-swarm", but this time the connotations are far from pleasantly pastoral.

112

Another surprise is found in

> "... a leafshaped lake
> As good as any colour transparency".

Here normal values have been reversed, and the man-made object, not nature, is seen as the yardstick by which we judge scenic beauty.

We have a very unusual collocation in "seen to death", suggesting both the destructive nature of tourism and the boredom of its modern participants. The artificiality which the poet finds distasteful in modern life is well brought out in "polythene cake" and in the colloquial "portable telly". In striking contrast to all of this is the strongly emphasised "Awed" which opens the last line.

"Bavelaw in Winter" is so full of striking language features that only a few examples can be mentioned. The scene which sparks off the poem is the sight of a reservoir shining through a row of trees. The poet compares this to

> "A cretin's gaptoothed grin through which
> Cold winds drew breath for bleak syllables
> On the subject of desolation".

It is an ugly and unpleasant image, particularly if we consider the effect of "cretin's gaptoothed grin" and the words "cold", "bleak" and "desolation". Similar unpleasant associations are found in "pewter clouds" which "mangled" the sky as they raced over "skull-shaped hills".

Later we have the names of various prehistoric animals such as mastodon, pterodactyl and tyrannosaurus rex, and associated with them is a Biblical reference to Golgotha, the "place of skulls" which was the hill of execution in old Jerusalem. Druids too are referred to, with the hint of unpleasant ritual often associated with the name. This whole passage of the poem thus conjures up a sense of terrifying violence.

But suddenly we return to the prosaic world of the present with

> "And now asthmatic sheep turn up collars
> Against the winds of night".

Nothing could be in sharper contrast to the frightening scene earlier imagined than these real-life sheep, "asthmatic" at that, who figuratively "turn up collars". The poem then finishes with two lines of simple, even humdrum language as the poet makes his way home.

Sound Effects

Sound makes a very important contribution to most poetry. Often poetry is based on regularly recurring echoes of sound, such as rhyming effects, or regularly recurring rhythms. There are in addition other sound effects such as onomatopoeia, alliteration, and pauses in the sound which can help focus attention on something important. Onomatopoeia and alliteration have already been described.

A regular system of rhyme occurs in many poems, but it is not an essential feature. Sometimes no rhyme at all occurs, sometimes occasional rhyme, when the rhymed words are particularly important and the rhyme is used to make them stand out. There are several different sub-divisions of rhyme, all performing a similar function – full rhyme, half rhyme, pararhyme, mid-rhyme, assonance (rhyming of vowel sounds only), etc. Alliteration itself is also a form of rhyme. These are technicalities, however, which need not be known for the present purpose. Similarly, regular patterns of rhythm are very common, but are not invariably found. In a great deal of poetry there is no regular pattern but instead an underlying suggestion of different rhythms with again items of special importance being marked off by some kind of pattern of stress that is unusual in the context. The whole field of rhyme and rhythm is virtually a science in itself, with measurable units which can be identified in technical terminology – expressions such as iambic pentameter and anapaestic tetrameter. For our purposes, the details and the terminology are unimportant, though they are very useful if they are known.

Often we can find a significance in the point where a line stops and another one begins, for there is a natural pause here even if the sense appears to carry on into the next line, and the pause may be specially significant. The same is true of any pauses imposed on the reader of the poem by any use of punctuation, especially if stops occur inside a line.

These sound effects are what we shall look for now in our next examination of the two poems, although in neither case is rhyme present. In "Lake Scene", the isolation by pauses of the word "even" at the end of line 5 has already been referred to, as has the isolation of "Awed" at the beginning of the last line. One further point might be made about the latter case. Before this line there is a single sentence which begins on line 8 and continues to the full stop at the end of line 19. Thus the pause before "Awed" is a particularly emphatic one. Another example of a word being isolated by pauses is "framed" on line 13. The comma before the word indicates a brief pause, but there is also a momentary pause after the word since it is the last word in the line. Thus added emphasis is given to it, and we can see the connection between "colour transparency" on the previous line

114

and "windscreens" on the next. A very striking example occurs at the opening of the final stanza:

"Or stop – and out come . . ."

Alliteration is used on two occasions. One occurs in lines 5 and 6, where the enormity of the depredations of the car is heightened by the use of alliteration in "Pasture and ploughland" and "Homes and houses". The other occurs in line 10, already noted as an important line, where the repeated uses of the "s" sound is another device by which attention is drawn to the line.

A good example of well-used alliteration also occurs in "Bavelaw in Winter". Attention has already been drawn to the ugliness of the image in "A cretin's gaptoothed grin". Part of that ugliness is conveyed by the alliteration used.

There are several examples of onomatopoeia. In line 12, when the poet is beginning to imagine the moor as the haunt of violent prehistoric animals, he describes it as "the peat-hag riddled moor", but when a few lines later he refers to the actual creatures of the land he speaks of "the burbling curlew".

Unlike "Lake Scene", there is in "Bavelaw in Winter" something resembling a regular rhythmical pattern. There are many exceptions and irregularities, but broadly the pattern is one of four stresses in each line. (Technically, it is written in iambic tetrameter.) The only time when this becomes strikingly regular, however, is in the last two lines:

"I turn up mine and head for home
A Bronze Age cairn will keep till spring".

The poet's frightening experience is over. Everything is back to normal. Something of this normality is reflected in the regularity of these two lines.

Personal Evaluation

No more technical devices will be discussed here, although the ground is far from fully covered. We come now to the final step in Practical Criticism, and in many respects the most important – the arrival at a personal evaluation of the poem as an experience. The technicalities themselves are unimportant if they have not led to a deeper understanding of the poem and a greater response to it. This is what must somehow be brought out throughout the treatment of the questions, but especially towards the end. In the two poems we have been considering, the last question in each case will reveal this most of all.

At the end of the close study of a poem that is demanded in Practical Criticism, you should be aware of how much more you know and understand. You should be putting together all the jigsaw pieces which the individual questions represent in order to complete the picture, which you can now look at with new eyes. The whole poem should be read again with this new awareness and any additional nuances of meaning discovered. At the end of it all you should be able to say with confidence that this is a poem you know well.

SOME REMINDERS

This final short chapter will be devoted to some reminders of things which will be important to you while sitting the examination. They will be based entirely on what was said in the appropriate parts of the earlier chapters.

PAPER I

Question A

Choice of Subject: Something you know about. Something you have feelings or opinions about. A register you can handle.

Relevance: Ensure that your composition fully meets the requirements of the question.

Timing: **Devote 1 hour to Question A**
5 minutes choosing, 10 minutes planning, 40 minutes composing, 5 minutes revising.

Length: Aim to produce about 500–600 words.

Planning: General title: Paragraph sub-titles: Notes on the paragraphs.

Paragraph structure: Topic sentence: Amplification of the topic sentence: Re-statement of the topic.

Paragraph linkage: Use some linking device in the first sentence of each paragraph.

Sentence structure: Write in complete sentences. Introduce variety of sentence length and sentence structures.

Lexical choice: Use effective words appropriate to the situation. Avoid excessive use of the 'pathetic fallacy'. Avoid an excessively 'learned' vocabulary.

Description: Use narrative as a framework, but avoid mere story-telling.

Short Story: Choose an ending with a point to it. Establish your main character – one close to your experience. Introduce an event, not too sensational. Show its effect on your character. Use good dialogue.

Expression of opinion: Statement of attitude. Each argument presented in one paragraph. Refutation of the opposite viewpoint. Re-statement of attitude.

Reflective essay: A good paragraph plan is essential. It should lead to a firm conclusion.

Special registers: Make sure that you introduce some markers of the register required (article, speech, letter, etc.)

Question B

Interpretation of instructions: Be sure who is writing the report and for what purpose.

Selection of material: Discard anything irrelevant, but only if you are certain.

Organisation of material: Devise a paragraph plan. Group the material in a logical order, not the order in which it is presented to you. Paragraph headings should not be used in the report itself.

Tone: Who are you supposed to be?
What are you writing?
What is its purpose?
Who is the intended reader?

Expression: Write in correct style with no informality of language. No abbreviated forms are to be used. All the normal rules of good composition should be observed.

PAPER II

Answer briefly where possible, more fully when the number of marks offered indicates it. Within each main question, deal with each sub-question in the proper order.
You may decide to do Question B before Question A.
Allow about 75 minutes for Question A and 15 minutes for Question B. Remember throughout to use your own words wherever possible. Read each passage carefully at least twice before attempting the questions.

Question A

Section 1: Do not merely give the meanings of words and phrases: in each case answer exactly the question that is asked.

Section 2: The number of points to be dealt with can usually be deduced from the number of marks offered. Every part of every question should be dealt with.

Section 3: Allow about 2 minutes per mark for the summary. Draw up a plan as for composition. All notes in the plan should be in your own words. Paragraph titles should indicate the chief stages in the argument. Discard unnecessary material – repetition, figurative language, examples. Include only the author's viewpoint. Compose the summary from your notes, not from the passage. Aim to produce a good piece of prose which will read well and will be fully comprehensible without reference to the passage. Ensure that your summary is within the prescribed limits of length. If necessary make out a fair copy of the final summary and cross out everything else. Add in brackets the number of words used – accurately and honestly.

Section 4: Look for matters of imagery, connotation, collocation, grammar, punctuation etc. In all cases, questions must be studied closely to ensure that they are fully answered.

Question B

Remember that this deals with language variety and literary technique, not simply with meaning. Again, the questions must be read very carefully.

PAPER III

Allow equal time for each question – roughly 5 minutes to choose questions and then 30–35 minutes for each. One question should be selected at once from each of the first three sections before examining Section 4. If you decide to do this section, immediately discard one of the other three.

Sections 1, 2 and 3

Choosing the questions: Do you know a text which fits the exact demands of the question? Do you know it well enough? Did it make a strong impression on you?

Planning the answer: Devise a paragraph plan that will ensure relevance and adequate textual reference.

Composing the answer: Sincerity is essential: there must be no prepared answers.

The answer must be a good piece of composition. The key phrase of the question should figure in the opening sentence, and should appear thereafter in the topic sentence of each paragraph and at the end of the whole answer.

Quotations should be few, brief and apt. They should be properly introduced.

Thematic questions: Make sure that you deal adequately with a sufficient number of texts. Devote most attention to the major text, using minor texts to support your answer.

Technique questions: Make sure that you are dealing with technique, not with content.

Remember the importance of relevance. Answer the precise points raised in the questions.

Section 4

This question should be chosen only if you are aware of the nature of literary technique. All answers must be based on the words of the text and should refer to these words.

Situation: Who is speaking? To whom? In what circumstances? What register is used? Why? Is it maintained?

Grammar: All departures from normal conventions should be noticed and their effects considered.

Lexis: Look for word connotations, unusual collocations, visual imagery and ambiguity.

Sound: Look for rhyme, rhythm, alliteration, onomatopoeia, and pauses.

Personal evaluation: Try to ensure that, especially towards the end of the questions, you are able to give something of your overall reaction to the poem.

APPENDIX

QUESTION A

Choose ONE of the following topics and write a composition relevant to it. You may include an appropriate title for the guidance of the examiner. (You should spend about one hour on this question.)

Marks

(*a*) "But the times when we were happy
Were the times we never tried."

Write about the unplanned experiences that have given you happiness.   (35)

(*b*) "Places that have been good to us we love.
The rest we are resigned to."

What are your thoughts and feelings about **either** a place (home, school, town, holiday resort, etc.) that you are "resigned to" **or** a place that has been "good" to you?   (35)

(*c*) "There is nothing so distant as the previous decade."

What trends (for example moral, cultural, social, political, educational, etc.) do you expect to see develop in the 1980s as a reaction to the 1970s?   (35)

(*d*) "Children aren't happy with nothing to ignore,
And that's what parents were created for."

What do you think are the factors which help create the ideal parent/child relationship? What factors sometimes tend to spoil that relationship?   (35)

(*e*) Write descriptively about the scene and/or mood evoked by **one** of the following.

(A short story is **not** acceptable.)

(i) "A flash of lightning:
Into the gloom
Goes the heron's cry."

(ii) "The tram-car full,
'Stop shoving,' they shout,
And go on shoving."

(iii) "Winter rain:
A farmhouse piled with firewood,
A light in the window."

123

(iv) "Factory chimneys
Never make clouds
Quite like God's."

(35)

(f) Write a short story suggested by the ideas contained in **one** of the following:

(i) "Every silver lining has its cloud."

(ii) "It is not enough to succeed; others must fail."

(iii) "And now John realized that, whatever else, being adult meant the ability not just to be surprised, but the ability to cope with the surprises."

(iv) "The trouble with Thomas is he mistakes aggression for personality."

(35)

(g) "All man's wisdom is contained in imaginative literature."

Write an essay about the importance of reading in your life.

(35)

(h) It is fashionable at the moment to be against censorship of television, cinema, theatre or newspapers. Yet we live with censorship daily in that we carefully edit what we say to others to avoid all kinds of clashes and hurt. Argue for or against the case that in any moderate society there has to be censorship of the media.

(35)

(i) Someone once said that comedy is the gap between what we are in fact like and what we wish we were like. Write a humorous essay about yourself making clear how wide that gap is.

(35)

QUESTION B

Shirvaglen High School's Parents' Association have written to you, the Head Teacher, recommending that the wearing of school uniform be abolished. You consult your staff and a representative group of pupils before issuing a statement to all interested parties in which you will **(a) briefly outline the situation, (b) give a summary of the arguments for and against the wearing of school uniform and (c) weigh up these arguments and announce your final decision.**

You have before you a selection of comments from staff, pupils, Parents' Association meetings and your own notes. Using this material as effectively as you can, write out your statement in 250-300 words of formal, continuous prose. (Do not waste time in making a count since there is no penalty for exceeding this amount.)

EXTRACTS FROM TRANSCRIPT OF PARENTS' ASSOCIATION MEETING

Parent A: Let's face it, times have changed . . . the whole notion of school uniform's out of date. The kids don't want to wear it any more; most of them don't bother with it.

Parent B: What bothers me is the cost . . . it's just too dear. I can't afford it with three of them at the school. Jeans and cords are much cheaper.

Parent C: It's so thoroughly impractical. After all, they only ever wear it at school; the blazer is too warm in summer and too cold in winter. And it gets so terribly shabby.

Parent D: I think the most cogent argument against its retention is that it suppresses their individuality, encouraging a society of convergents and conformists.

Parent E: But they do look nice in it, as though they belong to the school. They should be proud to wear it.

Parent F: Well, they prefer casual clothes, and you won't change them. We must abandon it altogether.

Marks

EXTRACTS FROM TRANSCRIPT OF STAFF MEETING

Mr. B: Discipline is already deteriorating at an alarming rate. To abolish uniform now would be to speed up the process even more.

Miss R: What we need is a set of school rules – simplified, codified, circulated and *enforced*. Let's enforce uniform while we're at it.

Mr. A: But after all quite a few of us have given up suits and come to school casually. Why force pupils to do what we don't do?

Mr. G: We want our pupils to have pride in the school. That won't be achieved while there are kids in scruffy jeans. Casual clothes mean casual attitudes.

Mr. S: Let them wear what they feel most comfortable in. What advantage is there in uniformity?

EXTRACTS FROM INTERVIEWS WITH PUPILS

The well-off will just show off. The rest of us won't be able to keep up with them . . . We behave better especially on out-of-school trips when we're in uniform. They can't *make* us wear it . . . It's too restricting – we feel more at ease in ordinary clothes . . . You don't have to waste time making decisions in the morning about what to wear . . . It saves our good clothes for going out. Denim jackets and jeans are a kind of uniform anyway.

HEAD TEACHER'S NOTES

Must avoid a head-on collision with P.A. – need to be firm but tactful. Does iron out social differences, encourages equality, gets rid of that denim mentality, aids discipline. What's the alternative? Problem is, enforcement. Need for persuasion rather than coercion. Got to have good arguments.

(15)

HIGHER GRADE – (Paper II – Interpretation and Language)   Time 1½ hours

QUESTION A

Read the passage and then answer, **as far as possible in your own words,** the questions which follow:

Among scientists Einstein's genius had been both recognised and acknowledged for 14 years but it was only now that the public at large became aware of him. It is difficult to analyse the sources from which the world-wide fame of Einstein sprang so suddenly. The public was undoubtedly well aware that there were strange happenings in the traditionally
5 unshakeable temples of science; in Britain, for example, some of its most honoured scientists had had to acknowledge that the stature of its greatest scientific genius, Newton, had been bent in places by a German-Swiss clerk. Moreover the popular press found copy in Einstein and in the apparently far-reaching consequences of his theories. Newspaper photographers discovered a highly photogenic and, for a time at least, tolerant subject: his was a face of
10 character: drooping, kindly eyes and wrinkles of humour surrounded by a leonine mane of hair. The habits of the man were a little irregular; already some of the characteristics

125

expected of the absent-minded professor were beginning to show: he lived a simple life uncluttered by possessions and any of the outward trappings of success; when there was no need to be careful he was careless about his dress: sometimes he wore no socks.

15   All these qualities, combined with the publicised qualities of the man, kindliness, gentleness and warmth, would still not have been sufficient to turn Einstein into the international figure he was to become. The missing ingredient in this recipe for public fame was the apparently incomprehensible nature of Einstein's work. For a few years after the publication of the general theory of relativity only a limited number of scientists familiarised
20   themselves with it in detail. Its abstruse nature became legend and absurd stories sprang up around its esoteric significance. It was even rumoured that there were few men in the world who were capable of understanding the theory. One story had it that a newspaper reporter had approached Sir Arthur Eddington and said that he had heard that there were only three people who were truly able to understand Einstein's work. "Really?" was supposed to have
25   been Eddington's reply. "And who's the third?" Popularisations of relativity theory appeared in the newspapers and magazines of a world which, after four years of war, was delighted to read something other than stories of trenches, wounded, rehabilitation or peace conferences. In most cases the popularisers failed to remind their readers that if the author of relativity theory had been best able to express his work in non-mathematical language then
30   he would probably have done so. The satisfactory outcome of this great burst of popularisa-tion was that a part of physics, in the name of Einstein and in the word 'relativity', entered common culture. The tousle-haired man became the subject of cartoons, the butt of jokes ("Tell me Dr Einstein, what time does this station stop at the next train?"); and because of his singular casual Bohemian appearance he became the epitome of the scientist. The
35   unsatisfactory outcome of it all was that Einstein was assumed to have a deeper insight than other men into subjects of which he claimed no special knowledge. Vaguely it was known that his work had revolutionised scientists' concepts of space and time, and therefore it was believed that in some way Einstein was dabbling with space and time and perhaps even dabbling with things quite near to God. Whatever the nature of the reasons the result was
40   surprising: Einstein was the first scientist to become a world figure in his lifetime.

Section 1   *Marks*

(a)   The author uses in line 1 the world "*acknowledged*". In what way does this word extend the meaning of the sentence up to this point?   2

(b)   What points does the author wish to make about science when he uses the words "*unshakeable*" and "*temples*" in line 5?   2

(c)   What is the effect on meaning of the author's use of:

   (i) *for a time at least* (line 9) in the fifth sentence of paragraph 1;
   (ii) *apparently* (line 18) in the second sentence of paragraph 2?   2

(d)   What is meant by "*Its abstruse nature became legend*" (line 20)?   2

(e)   Examine the context (lines 30–34) of the following expression:
      common culture (line 32).
      Say what this expression means and explain how the **context** helped you to arrive at the meaning.   2

                                                                                             (10)

Section 2

(a)   Which one "*strange happening*" (line 4) in science is referred to by the author?   1

126

(*b*) Why, according to the information contained in lines 7–14, did the popular press   *Marks*
become interested

   (i) in Einstein's theories, and   1
   (ii) in the man himself?   3

(*c*) Examine carefully lines 15–30 and then answer the following:

   (i) Why, according to the author, did "*absurd stories*" (line 20) spring up about
Einstein's theory?   2
   (ii) What made the public at that time particularly receptive to the various
popularisations of Einstein's work?   1
   (iii) Why, according to the author, did these popularisations fail to elucidate Einstein's theory?   1

(*d*) In lines 30–39 the author considers the consequences of the popularisation
process.

   (i) In what ways, according to the author, could the outcome be said to be
satisfactory?   2
   (ii) A scientist, say, might not agree with the author that this outcome was
satisfactory. Why?   1
   (iii) What, according to the author, was the unsatisfactory outcome?   2

                   (14)

Section 3

Examine carefully lines 2–18 ("*It is difficult . . .*" to "*. . . apparently incomprehensible nature of Einstein's work.*")

In no more than 75 words, summarise the reasons put forward by the author for Einstein's rapid rise to public fame.   (6)

Section 4

(*a*) The author introduces into the second paragraph an anecdote about Sir Arthur
Eddington (lines 22–25) and a joke concerning Einstein (line 33). Choose
one or the other and say for what purpose the author includes it.   1

(*b*) "*. . . the stature of its greatest scientific genius, Newton, had been bent in places by a German-Swiss clerk.*" (line 6)

What effect is intended by the author in thus describing Newton and Einstein, and
how is that effect produced?   3

(*c*) "*sometimes he wore no socks.*" (line 14)

Suggest **two** reasons why this is an effective conclusion to the sentence beginning
on line 11.   2

(*d*) Demonstrate that the sentence beginning "*All these qualities . . .*" (lines 15–17)
performs an important linking function between the two paragraphs of the
passage.   2

(*e*) The word "*dabbling*" appears twice in the second last sentence of the passage.
Make clear what the author implies by his use of this word.   2

                   (10)

Read the following passage carefully and answer the question on it.

The Mem, or Schoolmistress

Miss Peerie, the schoolmistress, was, about sixty years ago, the most beautiful young woman in our town; her father was head-master of the grammar-school, and she excelled every young lady far and near in accomplishments. She danced, but it was only not to appear above human nature; everybody who saw her had no adjective by which her beauty could be
5 described; Greek and Latin were to her household words, and she could read Hebrew as easily as if it had been the A B C.

She was then blooming: the epithet bonny was never applied to a more suitable subject, and her temper was as mellow as her looks were sweet. She had such a sleight in dressing, that every thing she wore seemed to grow better on her than on any other young lady; and on
10 her every pattern, no matter how old-fashioned, seemed to improve in gaiety and beauty.

But marriages are made in heaven, and fortune is not at man's bidding. Years have passed away, her beauty departed, and her still more delightful temper become all odds and ends, like the contents of a wisdom-bag. Had the boldest soothsayer foretold her fate in that blithesome time, he would have been derided as envious and malignant; nor was it in the
15 heart of man to imagine she would ever become the lonely inhabitant of a garret-room, and exercise the rod of authority over negligent and giggling misses. And yet such came to pass: she lived in an attic, and followed the patient and penurious bread-making of a schoolmistress, until her failing sight obliged her to give up the teaching of white-seam with the hieroglyphicals of the sampler, and to addict herself in the twilight of old age entirely to
20 the knitting of stockings. But the course of life with Miss Peerie, if we except her school-mistressing, was not uncommon; though the world withholds its sympathy from many that equally deserve it. She was the victim of disappointments, and a low winter sun dawned upon her lot, which through all her days has only served to shew its bleakness.

John Galt

                                                              Marks

(a) *"Had the boldest soothsayer foretold her fate in that blithesome time, he would have been derided as envious and malignant;"* (lines 13–14)

Identify and comment on **one** language feature in these lines which might indicate that the passage is from **a pre-twentieth century** text.   2

(b) Consider carefully the first sentence of paragraph 3 and comment on its function in establishing the relationship between the first two paragraphs (lines 1–10) and the third (lines 11–23).   2

(c) *"the lonely inhabitant of a garret-room"* (line 15)
     "exercise the rod of authority over negligent and giggling misses" (line 16)
     "patient and penurious bread-making" (line 17)
     "in the twilight of old age" (line 19)
     "she was the victim of disappointments" (line 22)
     "a low winter sun dawned upon her lot" (lines 22–23)

Examine carefully the word choice in any **three** of the above expressions, and demonstrate how the author enlists the reader's sympathy for Miss Peerie.   6

(10)

SECTION 1 – DRAMA

1. "A tragic situation exists precisely when virtue does **not** triumph but when it is still felt that man is nobler than the forces which destroy him."

    From any Shakespearean **tragedy** you have seen or read, demonstrate how "virtue does not triumph" and yet that the hero has qualities which make him "nobler than the forces which destroy him".

2. "It is very difficult to be wholly joyous or wholly sad on this earth. That which is comic, when it is human, soon takes upon itself the face of pain."

    What are the unhappy or painful episodes in any Shakespearean **comedy** you have read? In what way does Shakespeare use these episodes to create tension **or** uncertainty **or** suspense and how in the end is the unhappiness resolved, or left unresolved?

3. "The ending of any play must leave the audience satisfied that the outcome is the right one – one in which the characters are seen to be in the situation which their own words and actions have made inevitable."

    How far is this true of any play that you have read? Give a detailed account of the last part of the play and show whether or not the characters get what they deserve from their earlier words and actions.

4. Choose a play of any period which seems to you to deal with an issue affecting twentieth century society.

    EITHER:

    (*a*) Bring out clearly how the dramatist's attitudes to the issue are made clear by particular characters and/or scenes in the play.

    OR:

    (*b*) Compare the play with another text (which need **not** be a play) on the same issue and bring out the similarities and differences in the two writers' treatment of it.

5. You may have been involved recently in the production of a good play. You may, for example, have acted in it, or produced it, or had a part to play in the costume-design, in the lighting or the creation of sound effects. Write in detail about your particular contribution to the production.

SECTION 2 – PROSE

6. In reading a novel we very often come upon an incident which throws a new light on the significance of what we are reading, on what the novel is about. Give a brief account of such an incident from a novel you have read and discuss in what way it illuminated the rest of the book for you.

7. Choose a novel or short story set in Scotland in which the setting strongly influences how the characters live their lives. Describe this setting and show what part it plays in how different characters think, feel and act in the story.

8. In some novels the character who most threatens the hero is someone who cares for nothing except his own personal power or pleasure or advancement; in other novels he is someone who earns our grudging respect and even sympathy although we don't want him to succeed.

Bring out the nature of the hero's adversary in a novel you have read, showing in what way he/she is a danger to the hero and how in the end their conflict is worked out.

9.   "The essay is an instrument not only of pleasure but of reform."

Give a critical account of one (or more than one) essay by a single author which not only gives us pleasure but also attempts to alter our ideas **or** attitudes **or** values. The writer may be of the twentieth century or of an earlier period.

10.   In reading about other people's **real experiences** (whether in essay, biography, autobiography, reminiscence, travelogue or accounts of particular adventures) we are affected in different ways by those incidents which come close to our own experience and those that we could never imagine happening to us.

Examine the effect on you of reading such a work, bringing out which particular incidents **either** seemed very like experiences of your own **or** were totally outwith the likely scope of your own experience.

SECTION 3 – POETRY

11.   "The world is never the same once a good poem has been added to it. A good poem helps to change the shape and significance of the universe, helps to extend everyone's knowledge of himself and the world around him."

Choose a poem which did one or more of these things for you. Write about it in such a way as to reveal what gave it such a powerful effect.

12.   Write about the work of a Scottish poet who has a special appeal to you because he writes about a district of Scotland or an aspect of Scottish life with which you are familiar. You should examine at least **two** of his poems **in some detail,** drawing attention to the skill with which he illuminates his subject.

13.   "The first reading of a poem is like the opening and shutting of a door – we catch only a glimpse of what lies within. When we have time to read and reflect, so much more is revealed."

Write about what you first glimpsed in a particular poem which attracted you to it; and then about what later reading and study revealed.

14.   Some poems for their total effect depend upon unusual connections being made between different experiences, different objects, different words or images which startle us into seeing the familiar in new ways. By close reference to a poem of this kind you have read, demonstrate in what way the unusual connections contributed to your understanding of the poem.

15.   Choose a pre-twentieth century poem which reveals to us **either** something of the social life of its time **or** the personal pre-occupations of the poet. Examine how the poet goes about revealing **either** the nature of the society he lives in **or** his own private thoughts and feelings about his experience.

SECTION 4 – PRACTICAL CRITICISM

If you choose to do this section you should attempt all the questions in it.

16.   *This is a passage from a novel by Neil Gunn in which the narrator has come to a Mrs Maclellan to find out what had happened to another woman who had lived near her but who (some time before) had died in unusual circumstances.*

Read the passage carefully and then answer the questions which follow.

130

She smiled, the light in her grey-blue eyes. She was moved but not by what she told me so much as by what she had to tell me.

"Was she dark or fair?" I asked.

My interest made her feel she wasn't talking too much. She lifted her face with confidence
5 and some tinge of colour brought up a picture of her freckled youth.

"She was dark, but not black. I remember – it was some weeks after that first time – I remember coming out of the byre and seeing her down there by the burn humming an old air as she picked some primroses. The sun was shining on her hair and strands of it glistened with brown. It surprised me because I thought somehow she was quite dark. Her eyes were
10 brown, too, brown as the bottom of a hazel nut. It's funny how you don't notice most people's eyes. But her eyes looked at you. It was always such a pleasure to have her coming about the house. I went down to see the primroses. I said she had found them first, the first of the year. She lifted the little posy to her nose and her mouth couldn't laugh."

Mrs Maclellan glanced about her tea things to make sure I was being properly attended to.
15 She was putting off what she had to tell me, but the more she put it off the worse it was going to be for her. I may have been trained well enough in my job to know that emotion has its own truth and that you sometimes have to go an uncomfortable distance to find it.

"Where did she come from?" I asked.

QUESTIONS

Marks

(*a*) In the passage as a whole, identify any two signs that the "I" of the story (here-
after we will call him "the narrator") and Mrs Maclellan, although they have only
just met, are on good terms with one another.   3

(*b*) What are we meant to understand from the passage about Mrs Maclellan's
character?

In composing your answer you should take into careful account at least **three** of
the following:

the narrator's description of her (line 1 and lines 4,5);
the way she talks about the lady (lines 6–13);
what she says to the lady (line 12);
the way she finds it difficult to finish the story of what happened to the lady (lines
1,2 and lines 15–17).   6

(*c*) How does the writer gain our sympathy for the character of the lady?

In composing your answer you should take into careful account at least **two** of the
following:

Mrs Maclellan's description of her appearance (lines 6–10);
the sentence: "But her eyes looked at you." (line 11);
the sentence: "It was always such a pleasure to have her coming about the house."
(lines 11–12).   4

(*d*) Strong feeling is not easily expressed and may emerge in a roundabout way.
   (i) Quote the words which suggest this idea.   1
   (ii) How does his final question show that the narrator understands this idea? 2
   (iii) In the passage as a whole what other thoughts does the author give the
       narrator in order to make him seem a sensitive man?   4

(20)